CONTENTS

SOUND AND LIGHT 78

ELECTRICITY AND MAGNETS 114

FORCES AND MOTION

John Graham

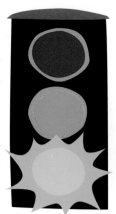

Getting started

Have you ever wondered why things move the way they do? What makes them start moving? Why do things fall when you drop them? Why is swimming so much harder than walking? You will discover answers to these questions, and many others, in this section of the book. It is packed full of experiments to try out at home or at school, which will help you to understand forces and motion.

Feel the force

Every time you ride a bike, turn the door handle or even just move your arm, you are using forces. They are the invisible pushes and pulls that make everything happen.

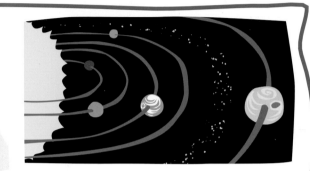

Athletes, dancers, racing drivers and builders all need to understand about forces. Every machine, from a playground see-saw to a space shuttle, relies on forces to work. From the tiny forces that hold atoms together to the huge forces that keep the planets going round the Sun, forces really are everywhere!

What you need

You can find most of the things you need for the activities in this section around your house or garage. If you do not happen to have exactly the item shown in the picture, you can probably use something similar that will do the same job. You may well find that you can improve on some of the ideas here. Improvisation is part of the fun of doing experiments!

Most of the activities use empty containers. Start saving plastic bottles, tubs and cartons. You never know what will come in handy!

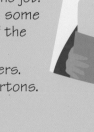

Your experiments are more likely to be successful if you work carefully and tidy up as you go along.

Warning

Read through all the steps for an activity before you start. Then work through them steadily – rushing or getting carried away could cause an accident. A pair of scissors or a hammer could cause serious injury. Ask an adult for help. Have fun, but work safely!

Take special care when using glue. Make sure you are using the right sort. Follow the instructions carefully and pay attention to any safety warnings. If in doubt, ask an adult.

Out of doors, stay away from traffic, open water, overhead power lines or other hazards. Make sure a responsible adult knows where you are and what you are doing.

Clock symbol

The clock symbol at the start of each experiment shows you approximately how many minutes the activity should take. All the experiments take between 5 and 30 minutes. If you are using glue, allow extra time for drying.

Having problems?

If something doesn't work properly at first, don't give up.

Look through the instructions and illustrations again to see if there's anything you've missed.

Some of the activities need patience – glue takes time to set and sometimes adjustments may be needed to get something to work well.

You don't have to do the experiments in the order they are in this section, although you may find they make a little more sense if you do. You don't have to do every single one, but the more you try out, the more you will discover about forces and motion, and the more fun you will have!

Stuck for words?

If you come across a word you don't understand, or you just want to find out a bit more, have a look in the Glossary on pages 150–157.

Measuring forces

Forces are all around us. They are the pushes and pulls that affect something's shape and how it moves. The strength of a force is measured in newtons (N), named after the English scientist and mathematician Sir Isaac Newton. On Earth, everything has weight. This is the force of gravity pulling things downward. In everyday life, people weigh things in 'kilograms' or 'pounds'. But because weight is a force, it should really be measured in newtons. On Earth, a 100g mass has a weight of 1N, and a 1kg mass a weight of 10N.

Make a force meter

It is easy to make a force meter which you can use to measure the force of gravity.

YOU WILL NEED 20
- A LARGE YOGHURT POT OR MARGARINE TUB
- STRING
- TWO BIG PAPER CLIPS
- A LONG, STRONG ELASTIC BAND
- PAPER, MARKER PEN AND A RULER
- A FEW FULL FOOD PACKETS WITH THEIR MASS IN GRAMS ON THEIR LABELS
- A SKEWER

1 Find a hook or peg somewhere, then attach a piece of paper to the wall underneath it. Loop the elastic band into a paper clip and hang the clip from the hook.

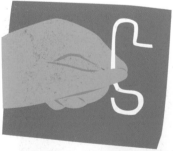

2 Open out the other paper clip to make a hook at one end and a pointer at the other. You may need some help and a pair of pliers.

3 Make holes around the rim of the pot. Use string to make a handle. Hang the pot from the elastic band with the bent paper clip.

4 Put the packets in the pot one at a time, and mark the position of the pointer each time to make a scale. Keep your eye level with the pointer. Do not overload the pot, or you will snap the elastic band! To turn your scale into newtons, remember that 100g weighs 1N, so 250g weighs 2.5N, 500g weighs 5N and so on.

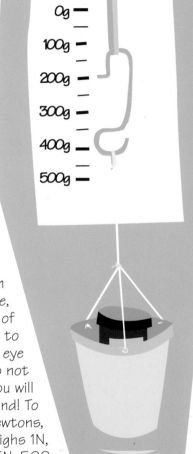

0g
100g
200g
300g
400g
500g

What's going on?

Things have weight because gravity pulls on them. The stronger the pull of gravity on an object, the more it weighs. Weight is really the force of gravity on something. The weighing machine works because the heavier a thing is, the further it stretches the elastic band.

Newton's apple

Big discoveries are sometimes made by chance. Sir Isaac Newton was a scientist who lived in England 300 years ago. The story goes that he was sitting in his garden when he saw an apple fall from a tree. He realised that there must be an invisible force pulling the apple down towards the Earth. He wondered if this force, called gravity, might affect the Moon, the stars and the planets as well. His ideas about gravity completely changed our understanding of the Universe.

ON A DIFFERENT SCALE

It's easy to work out your weight in newtons. Just multiply your mass (in kg) by 10. On the Moon, you would only weigh one sixth as much. Mass is the same everywhere, but weight depends on where you are.

Make a weighing scale

Put the large spring or sponge into the big tin, then the smaller tin on top. Put the bag of sugar into the smaller tin. Mark the smaller tin '10N' level with the edge of the bigger tin. Use other heavy things to make a scale. You could use kitchen scales to help you do this – remember 1kg weighs 10N.

YOU WILL NEED	10
◆ TWO DEEP EMPTY CAKE TINS, ONE SMALLER THAN THE OTHER	
◆ A LARGE SPRING FROM AN OLD MATTRESS OR CHAIR, OR A LARGE SPONGE	
◆ A 1KG BAG OF SUGAR	
◆ A WASHABLE MARKER PEN	

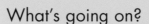

SUGAR
1KG

What happens to the spring when you put the objects in?

What's going on?

This time, instead of the force of gravity stretching an elastic band, it is squashing a spring. The more mass something has, the more strongly gravity pulls it down and the more the spring gets squashed.

Squeezing and twisting

Forces can make things change shape. Whenever something is bent, twisted, squashed or stretched a force is acting on it. Springy or elastic materials try to go back to their original shape when the force that made them change shape is taken away. This means they can store up energy and then release it to make things move. Wind-up toys and some watches work like this.

Wind-up toy

This intriguing toy shows how the energy stored in a twisted elastic band can cause movement. Ask an adult to find and break off the heads of a couple of safety matches for you.

YOU WILL NEED **20**
◆ A COTTON REEL
◆ A SMALL ELASTIC BAND
◆ HEADLESS SAFETY MATCHES
◆ STICKY TAPE
◆ A CANDLE
◆ A KNIFE
◆ A SKEWER

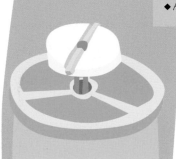

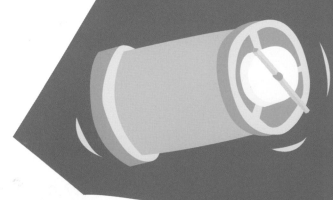

4 Wind up your toy by holding the reel and turning the long matchstick round and round. Put it down and watch it crawl!

1 Cut a thin slice from the wick end of the candle. Make the hole in the middle of the slice (where the wick was) big enough for the elastic band to fit through. Cut a groove in one side.

2 Poke the elastic band through the hole. Ask an adult for a headless matchstick, then put this through the loop and pull on the other end of the elastic band so the matchstick fits into the groove. Thread the long end of the elastic band through the reel.

3 Push half a matchstick through the loop of elastic band you have just pulled through. Stop it from turning, either with sticky tape or by wedging it with another half matchstick pushed into one of the holes in the reel.

What's going on?

As you use a turning force to twist the elastic band, you are storing up energy. Scientists call this potential energy. When you let go, the elastic band unwinds. This turns the matchstick leg and pushes the toy along. The potential energy in the twisted elastic band is turned back into movement energy.

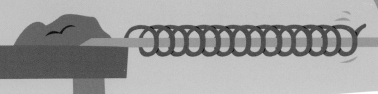

Spring launcher

Fix the stick to the edge of a table with a blob of modelling clay. Slide the spiral, and then the cotton reel, on to the stick. Press the reel down on the spiral and let go. How far can you make it fly? What happens if you give the reel more mass by sticking modelling clay to it?

What's going on?

The squashed spring pushes the reel, making it fly off the stick. The more mass the reel has, the greater the force that is needed to make it fly the same distance.

'Magic' rolling tin

Carefully make two holes in the lid and two holes in the bottom of the tin. Cut the elastic band then thread it through the holes and tie as shown. Tie on the weight where the elastic band crosses over and press the lid on. Now gently roll the tin forwards and let go.

YOU WILL NEED

10

- A LARGE CYLINDRICAL TIN WITH A LID
- A LONG ELASTIC BAND
- A HEAVY NUT OR SIMILAR WEIGHT
- STRING
- A HAMMER AND NAIL (ASK AN ADULT)

What happens when you let go of the tin?

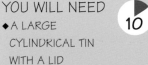

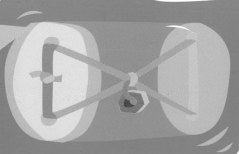

What's going on?

The tin comes back to you because the weight stays hanging below the elastic band, making it twist when you roll the tin. It is driven along by the potential energy stored up in the twisted rubber.

WIND-UP RADIO
This portable radio never needs batteries! Instead, it has a crank which is turned by hand to store energy in a big spring. As the spring slowly unwinds, it turns a little dynamo which powers the radio for about 20 minutes at a time. It is perfect for use anywhere remote.

Gravity

Everything is attracted to everything else by the force of gravity. The attraction between everyday things is too weak to notice. We only feel gravity pulling things down towards the ground so strongly because the Earth has a lot of mass. The more mass something has, the stronger its gravitational pull. The Moon has less mass, so gravity is weaker there. Nobody is quite sure what causes gravity, but without it we would all go flying off into space!

Anti-gravity cones

You would normally expect things to roll downhill. Or would you?

Do the cones appear to roll uphill or downhill?

YOU WILL NEED   10
- ◆ CARDBOARD
- ◆ TWO HALF CIRCLES OF THIN CARD
- ◆ A RULER AND PENCIL
- ◆ STICKY TAPE
- ◆ SCISSORS

1 Cut two pieces of cardboard into the shape shown. Tape the shortest sides together. Position the two pieces as shown.

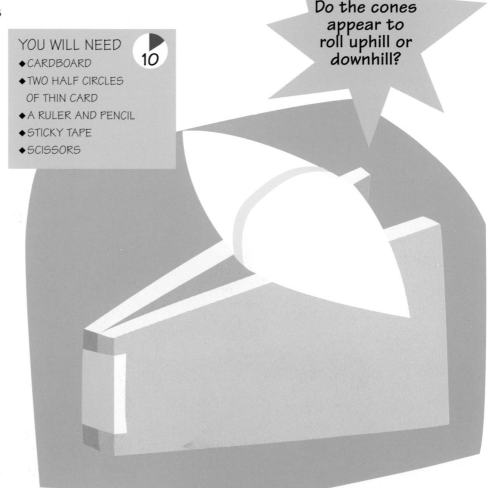

2 Roll and stick the half circles to make two matching cones. Tape the open ends together, as in the picture.

3 Put the cones at the bottom of the hill and watch them appear to defy gravity by rolling uphill!

What's going on?

The cones are not really defying gravity. They are actually going downhill. Watch the middle part carefully. Try measuring the distance from the middle of the cones to the ground at each end of the hill.

Do heavy things fall faster than light ones?

YOU WILL NEED

10

PAIRS OF THINGS THAT ARE THE SAME SIZE AND SHAPE, FOR EXAMPLE –
◆ A MARBLE AND A BALL BEARING
◆ A DICE AND A SUGAR CUBE
◆ A GOLF BALL AND A PING-PONG BALL
◆ TWO CAKE TIN LIDS OR BAKING TRAYS.

Find something safe to stand on, from which to drop your pairs of objects (a chair will do). Put the trays on the floor, one on either side of you. Drop both things from the same height at exactly the same time. Listen for them hitting the trays. Which one lands first? Try repeating your experiment to see if you get the same result every time.

Do the objects hit the trays at the same time?

What's going on?
Each pair should land together. Gravity makes them fall towards the Earth at the same rate, even though they weigh different amounts.

Galileo's story
In the 1590s, an Italian scientist called Galileo Galilei wondered if things would fall at the same speed regardless of how heavy they were. He tested his idea by dropping cannon balls of different weights from the Leaning Tower of Pisa. They always took the same time to hit the ground. His experiments got him into trouble with the Pope, who did not approve of his scientific approach to answering questions!

MOON LIGHT
This picture taken from a television transmission shows astronaut David Scott on the Moon in 1971. He took the opportunity to test Galileo's theory, this time with a feather and a hammer. There is no air on the Moon to slow down the feather, so sure enough they both hit the ground at the same time.

Balancing

Something does not have to be moving to have a force acting on it. Gravity is pulling on you now, even if you are sitting still. So what makes things fall over? Every object has a centre of gravity. This is the balancing point where the whole weight of the object seems to act. It affects how stable the object is. Things with a low centre of gravity are very stable. Things with a high centre of gravity tend to tip over.

The perching parrot

This parrot will stay on its perch, even when you try to tip it over!

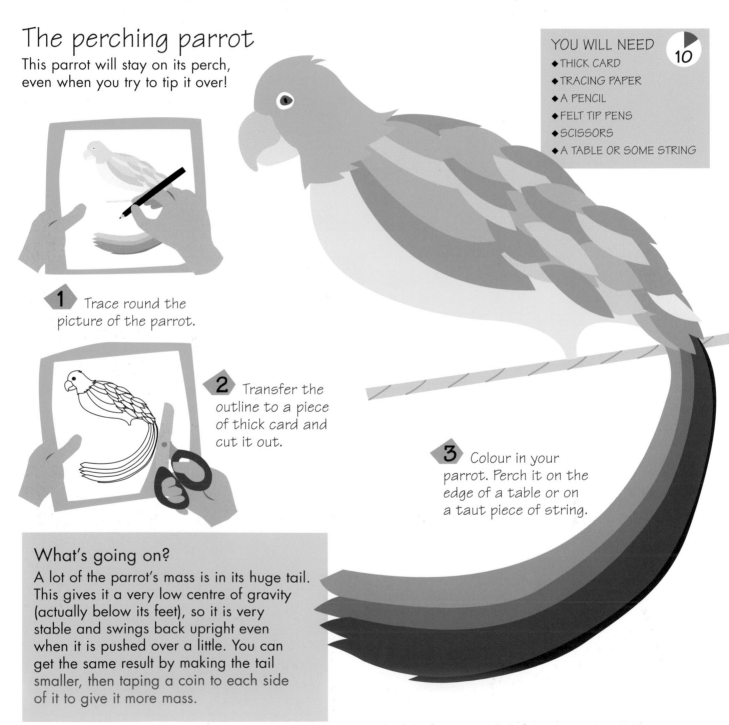

YOU WILL NEED

◆ THICK CARD
◆ TRACING PAPER
◆ A PENCIL
◆ FELT TIP PENS
◆ SCISSORS
◆ A TABLE OR SOME STRING

10

1 Trace round the picture of the parrot.

2 Transfer the outline to a piece of thick card and cut it out.

3 Colour in your parrot. Perch it on the edge of a table or on a taut piece of string.

What's going on?

A lot of the parrot's mass is in its huge tail. This gives it a very low centre of gravity (actually below its feet), so it is very stable and swings back upright even when it is pushed over a little. You can get the same result by making the tail smaller, then taping a coin to each side of it to give it more mass.

Balancing potato

Try to balance a potato on the tip of your finger. Tricky! Now push two forks into the potato at an angle, one either side. Try again. No problem!

What happens if you try using plastic forks?

What's going on?
The mass of the forks moves the potato's centre of gravity down lower, so that it balances. This does not happen when you use light plastic forks, because they do not have enough mass.

Magic box

Tape the weight into a corner of the box and put the lid on. Slide the box over the edge of a table until only the corner with the weight in it is on the table. The rest of the box seems to be held up by thin air! If you make a false bottom to hide the weight, you can even take the lid off to show that the box is 'empty'!

What's going on?
A box is a regular shape, so you would expect its centre of gravity to be in the middle. Adding the weight moves the centre of gravity towards the corner. So long as the box's centre of gravity is above the table, the box will not fall off. By the way, this also explains why the Leaning Tower of Pisa (page 15) does not tip over.

BALANCING ACT
This tightrope walker is holding a long, flexible pole to lower his centre of gravity and make him more stable on the narrow rope. Even so, this act still needs plenty of practice and a good head for heights!

Pressure

You can't push your thumb into a cork. But you can easily push a drawing pin into a cork using the same force. This is because the point of the drawing pin concentrates the force on to a tiny area, causing a lot of pressure. The pressure on your thumb is much lower, because the same force is spread out over the tack's big, flat head. The more a force is spread out, the lower the pressure.

Air pressure

The force of the air pressing on things is called air pressure. Although you can't see air pressure, you can see its effect with this quick experiment.

1 Fill the tumbler right up to the brim with water and slide the card over the top.

2 Hold the card against the tumbler with one hand. Get hold of the tumbler with your other hand.

YOU WILL NEED
- A PLASTIC TUMBLER
- A SINK
- A SHEET OF THIN, STIFF PLASTIC OR UNWANTED POSTCARD

5

3 Holding the card in place, turn the tumbler upside down over the sink. Let go of the card. It should stay put, held up by nothing but air pressure!

What's going on?

Air pressure pushes in all directions, including upwards. It is easily strong enough to hold up the weight of the water in a tumbler. The card acts as a seal, keeping the air out of the tumbler as you turn it upside down. In fact, the air is pressing in on every square centimetre of your body with a force of about 10N, the same as the weight of a 1kg bag of sugar. You are not crushed because your body is pushing back with an equal, opposite force.

Bed of nails

In 1969, a Hindu fakir named Silki stayed on a bed of nails for 111 days. The secret of his feat is all to do with pressure. Although each single nail has a sharp point, there are hundreds of them. The total area of all those points together is enough to reduce the pressure caused by the person's weight so that the nails do not do any harm. The only tricky bit is getting on and off!

Spread the force

Try pressing a coin into a lump of modelling clay with the flat side down. Then try pressing it in with the edge down. Which is easiest?

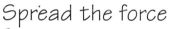

YOU WILL NEED ⑤
◆ A COIN
◆ MODELLING CLAY

What's going on?

The coin is much easier to push in on its edge. The smaller the area, the bigger the pressure caused by the force of your hand. The face has a much bigger area than the edge of the coin, so it spreads the force out and causes a lower pressure.

TRACTOR TYRES
This tractor's huge tyres do not just help it over rough terrain. By spreading its weight over a large area, they reduce the pressure so that the tractor does not sink into the soft ground.

Floating and sinking

Whether something floats or sinks depends on its density. This is a way of measuring how heavy something is for its size. A steel cube, for instance, is a lot heavier than a cube of ice of the same size. The steel cube will sink in water, but the ice cube floats. We say that ice is less dense than water, in other words a cube of ice weighs less than a cube of water the same size. So far so good, but how can a steel ship stay afloat?

Deep sea diver

You can see how changing something's density makes it float or sink by making this model of a diver.

YOU WILL NEED

20

- A TWO-LITRE PLASTIC DRINKS BOTTLE (WITH LID)
- A BENDY STRAW
- A PAPER CLIP
- AN ALUMINIUM PIE TIN
- RE-USABLE ADHESIVE
- SCISSORS
- A BOWL OF WATER

1 Cut out the shape of your diver from the pie tin. Make him tall and thin, about 7cm by 2cm, so he will fit through the neck of the bottle!

2 Bend the straw double, then cut it so you have a U-shaped piece about 2.5cm long. Slide the open ends of the straw on to the two ends of the paper clip.

3 Gently slide the paper clip and straw between the diver's legs and up on to his body. The straw should be on his back, bent at the top behind his head, looking like a real diver's air tanks.

4 Make diving boots out of re-usable adhesive and put them on his feet.

5 Try floating your diver in a bowl of water. Carefully adjust the amount of re-usable adhesive on his boots until he just floats.

6 Fill the bottle with water and put the diver inside. Make sure the bottle is full to overflowing then screw the lid on tightly. The diver should float to the top.

Can you make your diver float at any depth you like?

How does a boat float?

Test your objects to see which ones float and which sink. Drop a ball of modelling clay into the water. Flatten it out and make it into a bowl shape. Will it float now? Try the same with aluminium foil.

YOU WILL NEED

 10

- SOME SOLID OBJECTS MADE OUT OF DIFFERENT MATERIALS LIKE GLASS, METAL, WOOD AND PLASTIC
- MODELLING CLAY
- ALUMINIUM FOIL
- A LARGE BOWL OF WATER

How do the bowl shapes keep afloat?

What's going on?

Small, heavy things like coins and stones sink. Large, light things like corks float. But when you make a big, hollow boat shape out of something small and heavy like modelling clay, most of the boat is actually filled with air. Together, the boat and the air inside are less dense than water, so the boat floats. This is how ships can be made of steel.

7 Squeeze the bottle. The diver will sink to the bottom. Let go, and he'll float back up. With care, you can make him float at any depth you like!

What's going on?

When you squeeze the bottle, water is pushed into the straw. The air in the straw gets squeezed (compressed). This makes the diver heavier. His density increases, so he sinks. When you let go, the pressure of the air trapped in the straw pushes the water back out, making the diver less dense than water, so he floats up.

SWIMMING SHARK

Sharks are never still in the water but swim all the time. This is because they are denser than water, and if they stopped swimming they would sink.

Acceleration

Forces can make things speed up or accelerate. If the forces on something are balanced, it will not change speed. But if the force pushing an object forwards is greater than the force pushing it back, it will get faster and faster until the forces are in balance again. Unbalanced forces can make things change speed or direction.

Paddle boat

This paddle boat shows how unbalanced forces can push something forwards.

YOU WILL NEED
- ◆ A 2-LITRE PLASTIC DRINKS BOTTLE
- ◆ TWO STICKS ABOUT 23CM LONG
- ◆ PLASTIC CONTAINER WITH FLAT SIDES
- ◆ SCISSORS
- ◆ SOME WATERPROOF TAPE
- ◆ ELASTIC BAND, ABOUT 9CM LONG

20

1 Cut four rectangles from the flat sides of the plastic container, 5cm by 8cm each.

Can you make your boat go backwards?

2 Fold the rectangles in half and stand them on their long sides. Bring the folded edges together and secure them with tape to make a paddle.

5 Slide the paddle inside the elastic band and wind it up. Put your boat in a bath or pool of water, and let go!

3 Tape the two sticks to opposite sides of the bottle about three-quarters of the way down, so they stick out about 7cm.

4 Stretch the elastic band over the sticks. Use one that fits easily without being tightly stretched.

What's going on?

The boat is powered by the energy stored in the elastic band when you wind it up. As the paddle turns it pushes against the water, making the forces on the bottle unbalanced. It accelerates until the resistance of the water pushing back is equal to the force of the paddle pushing forwards and the forces are back in balance. Then it carries on at a steady speed until the elastic band runs out of stored energy.

Balloon boat

Soften the balloon by blowing it up a couple of times. Tape it to the straw and check that the seal is airtight. Make a small hole in one end of the tray, big enough for the straw to go through. Put the straw through the hole, blow up the balloon and seal the end of the straw with re-usable adhesive. Put the boat in some water and snip off the adhesive.

10

YOU WILL NEED
- A PLASTIC TRAY, THE SORT MICROWAVE MEALS COME IN
- A BENDY STRAW
- RE-USABLE ADHESIVE
- A BALLOON
- STICKY TAPE AND SCISSORS

What's going on?
The balloon pushes air out through the straw, which pushes the boat forwards. Jet engines and rockets work in just the same way, pushed forwards by gases shooting out at the back.

FLASHBACK

Land speed record
The first land speed record was set in 1898 by Count Gaston de Chasseloup-Laubat of Paris, France. His car took 57 seconds to cover a measured kilometre, averaging 63km/h. Almost 100 years later in 1997, the Thrust SSC supersonic car set a new record. Its twin turbojets accelerated Thrust SSC to an average speed of 1228km/h – faster than the speed of sound. The streamlined shape helped the car slice through the air with very little drag. Two sets of parachutes and special brakes were needed to bring it to rest.

SPRINTING CHEETAH
The cheetah holds the land speed record for animals. Its powerful legs and flexible spine allow it to accelerate to around 100km/h.

Measuring speed

Measuring speed can be very useful. Car drivers, for example, need to know if they are keeping below the speed limit. Train drivers need to know if they are going at the right speed to get to the next station at the right time. To work out how fast something is going, you need to know two things – the distance it has travelled and the time it has taken to do it.

Speed trial

Here is an easy way to measure how fast a cyclist is going. Ask an adult to find you a safe, traffic-free cycle path for this experiment.

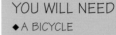

YOU WILL NEED
- A BICYCLE
- A STOPWATCH, OR WATCH WITH A SECOND HAND
- A MEASURING TAPE
- A CALCULATOR
- A FRIEND

10

Can you work out how fast you cycle?

1 Measure the distance between two things along the side of the path (trees, for example). Try to choose things about 50m apart.

2 Take a long 'run-up' so that you are cycling at a steady speed when you pass the first post. Get your friend to time how long it takes you to travel from the first post to the second post.

$$\text{average speed} = \frac{\text{distance travelled}}{\text{time taken}}$$

What's going on?

Average speed tells you how far the cyclist goes each second. For example, if the cyclist goes 50 metres in 5 seconds, her average speed is 50/5, which is 10 metres per second or 10 m/s. Speed is often measured in kilometres per hour (kph) or miles per hour (mph), but the idea is the same.

3 Use this equation to work out how fast you were going. If you measure the distance in metres and time in seconds, the answer will be in metres per second, or m/s for short.

Balloon rocket race

Cut a few straws into 10cm lengths. Thread them on to the end of the string. Tie the string between two chairs 10m apart, pulling it tight. Blow up a balloon. Pinch the neck tightly, then get a friend to tape it to the first piece of straw. Get your stopwatch ready, and let go! Time how long the balloon takes to fly to the other end of the string. Compare different shapes of balloon to see which goes fastest.

20

Can you work out the average speed of your balloon rockets?

What's going on?

The balloon squeezes the air inside, forcing it out of the end. This pushes the balloon forwards. Long, thin balloons fly faster than round ones because they are a more streamlined shape and have to push less air out of the way as they go forwards.

FLASHBACK

The hare and the tortoise

In this famous ancient Greek fable, a hare challenges a tortoise to a race. The tortoise accepts, and the race begins. The hare zooms off into the distance, but then stops for a nap. Meanwhile, the tortoise plods along steadily. When the hare wakes up, the tortoise is just about to pass the winning post and the hare loses the race. Although the hare's maximum speed was far faster, his average speed over the whole race was slower than the tortoise's.

PHOTO FINISH?

When 1/100th of a second can make the difference between gold and silver, an invisible beam linked to special cameras records each runner's time more accurately than a person with a stopwatch ever could.

Friction

Whenever things rub together, friction is produced. It is an invisible force that tries to stop movement. Friction also happens when something moves through a fluid like water or air. Then it is often called 'drag'. Sometimes friction is a useful force that provides grip or slows something down, but at other times it is a nuisance. Think about a bicycle – you lubricate moving parts like the chain to reduce friction, but you would be making a big mistake to put oil on the wheel rims where the brake pads rub!

Slide or grip?

This quick experiment shows how the amount of friction between two surfaces depends on how rough or smooth they are.

YOU WILL NEED
- A LARGE WOODEN BOARD
- A SMOOTH PLASTIC TRAY
- AN ASSORTMENT OF FLAT-BOTTOMED OBJECTS THAT WON'T BREAK EASILY, EG A PLASTIC CUP, COIN, RUBBER, MATCHBOX

10

Why do some things slide more easily than others?

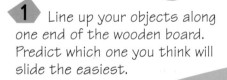

1 Line up your objects along one end of the wooden board. Predict which one you think will slide the easiest.

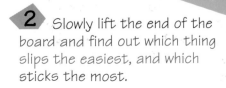

2 Slowly lift the end of the board and find out which thing slips the easiest, and which sticks the most.

3 Now try using the plastic tray. Does it make a difference?

What's going on?

Some things slide along the wooden board more easily than others because there is less friction between their bottom surface and the board. They will probably be the objects that feel smoother to the touch. Things slide much more easily along a smooth surface like the plastic tray for the same reason.

Slippery ice

Try sliding your objects along the table one by one. Now try the same with an ice cube. What do you notice?

How can water act as a lubricant?

YOU WILL NEED
◆ YOUR FLAT-BOTTOMED OBJECTS FROM 'SLIDE OR GRIP'
◆ A SMOOTH KITCHEN TABLE
◆ AN ICE CUBE

10

What's going on?
A thin layer of water from the melting ice reduces the amount of friction between the ice cube and the table, so it travels much more easily. The water acts as a lubricant, like the grease and oil between the moving parts of a machine. Water wouldn't normally be any good as a lubricant in a machine, though, because it would soon evaporate away and might make the machine parts go rusty!

Rubbing hands

Try rubbing the palms of your hands together, at first quite gently and slowly, then harder and more quickly. What do you notice? Make them wet and soapy, then try the same thing again.

YOU WILL NEED
◆ YOUR HANDS!
◆ SOAP AND WATER

5

What's going on?
The harder you press your hands together and the faster you rub, the hotter they feel. This is because rubbing your hands produces friction, and friction causes heat. When you do the same thing with wet, soapy hands, the water reduces the friction and so your hands feel less hot.

ICE SKATER
The narrow blade on the skate causes very high pressure underneath. This melts the ice, making a thin layer of water which lubricates the blade just like oil. There is very little friction left to slow the skater down.

Air and water resistance

It takes a lot of effort to swim. This is because you have to push the water out of your way as you move forwards. Then there's the friction of the water sliding against your skin, and the swirling water behind you trying to pull you back. Air has the same dragging effect, but you have to go faster before you really start to notice it. Drag isn't all bad, however. If your arms and legs slid through the water without any resistance, you wouldn't be able to push yourself forwards in the first place!

Make a parachute

See how a simple parachute slows a falling object. Get an adult to help you to get the strings all the same length.

YOU WILL NEED
◆ A PLASTIC BAG
◆ COTTON THREAD
◆ SCISSORS
◆ A PAPER CLIP
◆ A HOLE PUNCH
◆ MODELLING CLAY TO USE AS A WEIGHT, OR A SMALL TOY TO BE YOUR PARACHUTIST

20

How can a parachute slow something down as it falls?

2 Tie a 40cm length of thread to each corner.

1 Cut out a 30cm square from the plastic bag and punch a hole close to each corner.

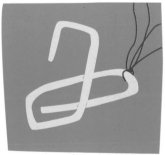

3 Tie the loose ends to the paper clip and add some modelling clay, or bend the paper clip to make a harness for your parachutist.

4 Drop the parachute from a safe height and see how long it takes to fall.

What's going on?

Parachutes work by causing as much air resistance as possible. The big, curved canopy traps air underneath which pushes up against it as it falls. The faster the parachute falls, the bigger the upwards force trying to slow it down again.

Air resistance

Stand in a space and try dropping your light objects one by one. Notice how they fall. Now get your sheets of paper tissue and screw one of them into a ball. Drop the sheet and the ball at the same time. What happens?

Why do some things fall faster than others?

YOU WILL NEED
5
◆ SEVERAL SMALL, LIGHT OBJECTS WHICH HAVE BIG SURFACES FOR THEIR WEIGHT, EG A FEATHER, A LEAF, A PIECE OF THREAD
◆ TWO SHEETS OF PAPER TISSUE

What's going on?

Things speed up when you drop them, then fall at a steady speed until they reach the ground. The screwed-up paper has a smaller surface area than the sheet. It moves through the air easily, and so falls quickly. The sheet has to push a lot more air out of its way. This extra air resistance makes it float down slowly.

Water resistance

Put both the balls into the bowl of water, so that they float. Try spinning first one, and then the other. Which spins more easily?

YOU WILL NEED
5
◆ A TENNIS BALL
◆ A BOWL OF WATER
◆ A SMOOTH RUBBER BALL

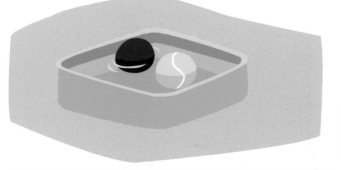

What's going on?

Water resists movement even more than air. The rubber ball spins more easily because its smooth surface does not cause as much drag as the rough tennis ball.

PARACHUTIST
When a parachute starts to fall, it accelerates until the upwards force of air resistance balances the pull of gravity. It then carries on falling at a steady speed called its 'terminal velocity'.

Floating in air

Because you cannot see it, it is easy to forget that air has weight. In fact, the atmosphere weighs a lot – try the air pressure experiment on page 18. Just like water, air causes an upwards force on things, called 'upthrust'. Believe it or not, if you put a weight on some scales and then take the air away, it will weigh more, in the same way that you weigh more when you let the water out of your bath. Something will float in air, just as in water, if the upthrust on it is equal to or more than its weight.

Make a hot air balloon

This balloon is quite tricky to make, but loads of fun! Ask an adult for help. Once you have made a working model you can scale it up to make a really big one.

YOU WILL NEED
◆ SHEETS OF TISSUE PAPER
◆ SCISSORS
◆ GLUE
◆ A HAIRDRYER
◆ BENDY STRAWS

20

1 Make a template, and then cut out eight pieces of tissue paper in the shape shown.

2 Using as little glue as you can, stick the edges together to make a balloon shape. It does not matter if you have to scrunch up the tissue a little to get it into the right shape, as long as there are no gaps left along the joins. A round patch of tissue will seal any gaps at the top.

3 Ask an adult to fill the balloon with hot air using the hairdryer. If it flips upside down, strengthen the hole by sticking in some bendy straws around the opening.

What makes your balloon fly?

What's going on?
Heating the air inside the balloon makes the air expand, pushing some out of the bottom. Now less air is taking up the same space, so it is less dense. The upthrust caused by the cooler, heavier air around the balloon makes it float upwards. As it cools down, the air in the balloon gets denser and heavier again, so the balloon comes down.

Hovering helium

Make lots of identical weights by cutting up aluminium trays into, say, squares 2cm x 2cm. Using a straightened paper clip, carefully poke a hole through one corner of each weight. Tie a paper clip to the helium balloon with string, and bend it to make a hanger for your aluminium weights. Attach weights one at a time until the balloon can only just lift them. Every hour or so you will have to take some weights off to keep the balloon in the air.

YOU WILL NEED
10
- ◆ A FRESHLY FILLED HELIUM BALLOON (THE SORT THAT FLOATS UP TO THE CEILING)
- ◆ PAPER CLIPS
- ◆ STRING
- ◆ SOME EMPTY ALUMINIUM FOOD TRAYS

What's going on?
Air is a mixture of gases, mostly nitrogen and oxygen, which are heavier than helium, which is a very light gas. A helium-filled balloon is lighter than air and floats upwards. The molecules of helium are so tiny, though, that after a while they start to leak out. The shrinking balloon gets heavier than air and gravity pulls it back down.

FLASHBACK

The deck chair pilot
In 1982 one-time pilot Larry Walters decided to fly once more. He tied 45 helium-filled weather balloons to a garden chair and took off, hoping to float just above the ground. Instead, he shot into the sky to a height of 3,200m. After 14 cold, terrifying hours he drifted past an airliner, whose pilot reported seeing a man on a garden chair at 3,000m! Mr Walters was blown out to sea where he was finally rescued by a helicopter, which towed him to safety.

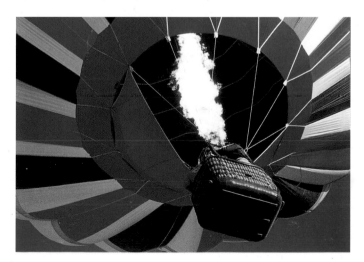

A HOT AIR BALLOON
A powerful burner heats the air inside the balloon. The cooler, denser air outside the balloon causes upthrust, lifting the balloon skywards. Regular blasts of heat will be needed to keep the balloon floating in the air.

Flight

There are other ways to create upwards forces on things to make them fly, apart from using hot air or a light gas like helium. Birds and flying insects use flapping wings to give them lift, pushing the air down and backwards to move forwards through the air. Aeroplanes use the same idea, but have fixed wings and propellers or jet engines to push them forwards. The lift comes from the shape of the wings. Rockets work by blasting hot gases from the tail which push the rocket forwards, even in the airless vacuum of space.

Make a rocket

This water rocket is great fun, but you will need an adult to help make it and supervise the launch.

25

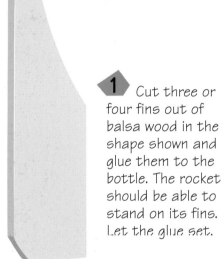

1 Cut three or four fins out of balsa wood in the shape shown and glue them to the bottle. The rocket should be able to stand on its fins. Let the glue set.

3 Fill the bottle about a quarter full with water and push the cork in hard.

2 Ask an adult to drill a small hole through the cork and push the needle adaptor in from the wide end. It needs to be a tight fit.

4 Take your rocket into the middle of an open space like a playing field, far away from buildings or overhead wires. Attach the connector and bicycle pump. Pump air into the bottle, keeping well back. Pressure will build up until the cork pops out and the rocket blasts off!

Make a glider

Follow the diagrams to fold the paper. Add a paper clip to the nose, then throw your glider gently. Experiment by moving the paper clip to see which position makes the glider fly the furthest.

YOU WILL NEED
◆ A SHEET OF PAPER
◆ A PAPER CLIP
10

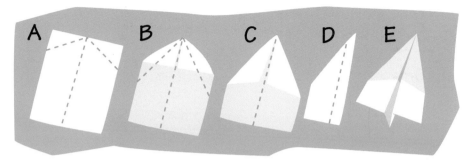

A   B   C   D   E

What's going on?

The glider flies a long way because of air resistance pushing up against the flat wings, opposing the pull of gravity.

Make a gyrocopter

Draw out the shape shown. Cut the side strips and fold them out to make the wings. Attach a paper clip to the bottom of your gyrocopter, then throw it up into the air.

YOU WILL NEED
◆ PAPER OR THIN CARD
◆ A PENCIL AND RULER
◆ SCISSORS
◆ A PAPER CLIP
10

What happens if you make one twice as big?

What's going on?

A gyrocopter is a helicopter without a motor. Air resistance causes the wings to spin as it falls. The spinning wings create lift which works in the opposite direction to gravity, slowing down its fall. Sycamore trees use the same trick to spread their seeds. The bigger the gyrocopter, the slower it falls.

What's going on?

Pumping air into the bottle increases the pressure inside until it overcomes the friction holding the cork in the neck of the bottle. The air and water blasting out of the bottom causes a reaction force which pushes the rocket upwards into the sky.

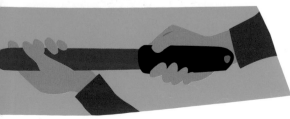

CRUISING CONDOR
Birds are masters of flight. Condors like this one flap their wings to take off and gain height. They can then glide for long distances. The shape of their wings gives them lift, and they can ride on rising columns of warmer air, called thermals, for hours.

Force magnifiers

Levers and pulleys are 'force magnifiers'. How would you get the lid off a can of paint? You could use a screwdriver or something similar as a lever. Think about a door handle. You push the handle a long way to make the latch move only a little to open the door. These are 'force magnifiers'. A small force is used to move one end a long way, causing a big force to move something a short distance at the other end.

Pulley power

Delight your friends and worry your enemies with this demonstration of your superhuman strength!

YOU WILL NEED
◆ TWO BROOMS OR MOPS
◆ A FEW METRES OF ROPE
◆ SOME TALC
◆ A FEW FRIENDS
10

1 Tie the rope near the end of one broom.

2 Dust the two broom handles with talcum powder to reduce friction.

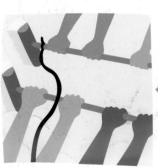

3 Get two or even four friends to hold the two brooms apart.

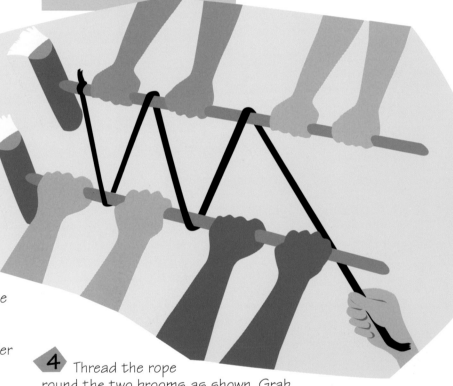

4 Thread the rope round the two brooms as shown. Grab hold of the free end of the rope. Tell your friends to try and keep the brooms apart with all their strength while you effortlessly pull them together!

What's going on?
Because of the way the rope is threaded between the brooms, pulling the free end a long way with a small force causes a huge force to tug the brooms a little way together. The broom handles are acting like pulleys. The more times the rope loops back and forth, the greater the force magnifying effect.

Make a double pulley

Ask an adult to cut a coat hanger into two pieces and bend them to hold the cotton reels and toy bucket as shown. Hang the wire without the bucket from a hook, attach the string as shown then thread it round all the pulleys. Try lifting some weights with your double pulley.

YOU WILL NEED 20
- FOUR COTTON REELS
- A WIRE COAT HANGER
- STRING
- A TOY BUCKET AND SOME THINGS TO PUT IN IT
- WIRE CUTTERS

How can you lift the bucket using the double pulley?

What's going on?
The double pulley works just like the broom trick. Pulling the string a long way with a small force lifts the weight a little way with a big force, so the bucket is easy to lift.

Levers

Ask an adult to bang the lid on to the tin so that it's really tight. Try levering it off, first with the handle of a teaspoon then with the dessert spoon handle. Take care not to bend the spoons!

YOU WILL NEED 5
- A TIN WITH A TIGHT LID, LIKE A COCOA TIN
- A TEASPOON
- A DESSERT SPOON

What's going on?
The longer a lever is, the greater the turning force it can cause. The spoon handle is the lever and the rim of the tin is the pivot. When you press on the spoon, your hand moves a long way with a small force. The end of the handle pushes the lid up a small way with a big force.

LOAD LIFTER
A wheelbarrow is a force magnifier. The wheel is the pivot and the handles are the lever. By lifting the handles a long distance with a small force, you can lift a heavy load just off the ground with a big force.

Gears

Gears are wheels with teeth round the outside. They can be connected directly together or joined by a chain. Depending on the sizes of the gear wheels, gears can be used as force magnifiers or movement magnifiers. They are used in all sorts of machines to change the speed or direction of movement. Bicycles and cars need gears to cope with going up and down hills and travelling at different speeds.

Bicycle gears

This experiment will show you the effect that gears have on a bicycle's movement.

1 Put the bicycle into its lowest gear.

2 Make a chalk mark on the path next to the back wheel, where it touches the ground.

3 Gently turn the pedals once, walking the bicycle forwards in a straight line. Make a second mark next to the back wheel. Measure the distance between the marks.

How do bicycle gears work?

4 Put the bicycle into top gear and repeat the experiment. How far does it go this time?

YOU WILL NEED
- A BICYCLE WITH GEARS
- A TAPE MEASURE
- SOME CHALK
- A QUIET, LEVEL PATH AWAY FROM ANY TRAFFIC

10

What's going on?

Bottom gear works as a force magnifier. It is very slow on flat ground, but good for climbing hills. The pedals go round quickly compared to the wheel. Top gear is for pedalling downhill or going fast on the level. The wheel goes round quickly compared to the pedals, but with much less power.

Making gears

Mark the centre of each lid and ask an adult to punch a hole through. Glue a cotton reel on to each lid in line with the hole. Stretch a thick elastic band round the rim of each lid to give them grip. Push two nails through the card, spaced so that when you slot two lids over them their rims just touch. Turn the larger lid and see how the smaller lid moves. Try some different combinations of lid sizes – you could even arrange three lids in a row. You will have to move the nails each time you change lid.

What's going on?

This is just like the top gear on a bicycle, only without the chain to link the two gear wheels. Turning the large wheel slowly makes the small wheel spin quickly, without much force, in the opposite direction. You can change it into a model of bottom gear by using the small wheel to turn the larger wheel. Now the big wheel turns slowly with a lot of force.

FLASHBACK

Harrison's chronometer

Gears are not only useful on big machines like bicycles. The mechanism of a clock uses precision gears to steadily turn the hands at exactly the right speed. The first really reliable portable clock, the H4 chronometer, was built nearly 250 years ago by English watchmaker John Harrison. With its intricate mechanism of gears and springs, H4 could keep good time, even on a ship at sea. This was a huge breakthrough. By keeping accurate track of the time, sailors could work out their precise position. It took Harrison 40 years to develop the H4, but it was worth it as he was awarded £18,000 for his achievement.

SPEED BIKE
Chris Boardman won Olympic gold in 1992 riding this very light superbike. The chainring cog is much bigger than the cog on the back wheel, giving very high gearing. The bike and rider have a streamlined shape, helping them to glide easily through the air.

Circular motion

Anything spinning around has circular motion. Remember that moving things will always go in a straight line unless there is a force tugging them off course. When something moves in a circle, it is constantly changing direction. For this to happen, there has to be a force pulling it towards the middle of the circle. Scientists call this centripetal force. You can easily feel this force on a playground roundabout, tugging on your arms as your body tries to fly off in a straight line!

Spinning force

This experiment shows how centripetal force increases the faster something spins round. Find a space away from anyone else to do this!

YOU WILL NEED
- A CORK OR RUBBER BUNG 10
- ABOUT 1M OF STRING
- A COTTON REEL
- A SMALL WEIGHT, LIKE A WOODEN BLOCK
- A DRILL (ASK AN ADULT)

What happens to the weight when the cork whirls round?

1 Ask an adult to drill a small hole lengthwise through the cork.

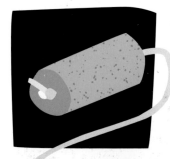

2 Thread one end of the string through the cork and tie a big enough knot in the end to stop the cork sliding off.

4 Hold the cotton reel. Start whirling the cork round in a circle, slowly at first and then faster and faster.

3 Thread the other end of the string through the cotton reel and tie it to the weight.

What's going on?

As the cork spins faster, the centripetal force needed to keep it going round in a circle instead of flying off in a straight line increases. This force tugs on the string, lifting the weight up. The faster you spin the cork, the higher the weight is lifted.

Make a spinner

Draw a circle on the card and cut it out. Carefully push the pointed end of a pencil through the centre of the circle. Spin the pencil on a smooth, flat surface.

YOU WILL NEED ▶ 10
- CARD OR THIN, STIFF PLASTIC
- A PAIR OF COMPASSES
- SCISSORS
- A PENCIL

What's going on?
Spinning objects like wheels and gyroscopes resist being tilted. This makes them very stable. The spinner will make the pencil balance on its point, especially if the centre of gravity is kept low by having the card low down on the pencil.

Anti-gravity water

Tie the string to the bucket's handle. Half fill the bucket with water. Hold the string and lift the bucket so that it hangs just above the ground. Start turning round, very slowly at first, then spin faster and faster. Watch what happens to the water as the bucket moves up higher.

YOU WILL NEED ▶ 10
- A SMALL BUCKET WITH A HANDLE
- STRONG STRING OR ROPE
- AN OPEN SPACE OUTDOORS

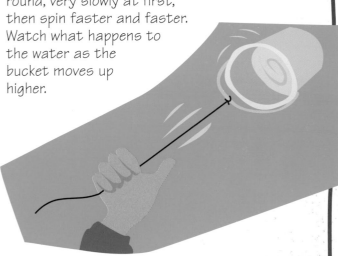

What's going on?
Centripetal force affects liquids, too. As the bucket spins, the water is trying to go in a straight line. The bottom of the bucket keeps pushing the water in towards the middle of the circle and the water gets pressed against the bottom of the bucket, so it can't spill out. The water stays inside the bucket, even when the bucket is on its side!

A FAIRGROUND RIDE
Spinning fairground rides work by upsetting your sense of gravity. This one spins you round, like the bucket of water, so that you can't tell up from down. Your body is trying to fly off in a straight line, but the ride is pulling you round and round in a circle.

Starting and stopping

It takes a push or a pull to start something moving or to make it stop. Imagine pushing a heavy shopping trolley. You have to push hard to start it moving, but once you've got it going it will keep going by itself even if you let go. You have to pull back on the handle to make it stop. This tendency of things to keep still if they're still, or keep moving if they're already moving, is called inertia. The more mass something has, the greater its inertia.

Don't lose your marbles

This simple experiment shows how inertia affects the motion of some marbles in a shoe box lid. You will need to use a smooth level floor.

YOU WILL NEED
◆ A FEW MARBLES OF VARIOUS SIZES
◆ A SHOE BOX LID
◆ STICKY TAPE
◆ A SKATEBOARD OR TOY WITH WHEELS

10

4 Watch the marbles as you stop the skateboard by pulling back on it.

What happens if the skateboard stops suddenly?

1 Use tape to stick the lid firmly to the top of the skateboard and put it on the floor.

2 Position the marbles in the lid so they are spaced apart from one another.

3 Start the skateboard moving by pushing it gently. Watch carefully what happens to the marbles.

What's going on?

Because they have inertia, the marbles try to stay still as you push the skateboard forwards. They only start moving when the back wall of the lid gives them a push. When the skateboard stops, they try to carry on moving forwards and roll to the front of the lid. The heavier the marble is, the more inertia it has and the more it resists any change in its motion.

Spinning egg puzzle

You can use this trick of inertia to find out if an egg is raw or cooked. Spin the cooked egg and then stop it spinning by gently grabbing it. Let go straight away. It will stop, like you would expect. Try the same with the raw egg. After you've stopped it and let go, it starts spinning again!

YOU WILL NEED
10
◆ A HARD-BOILED EGG
◆ A RAW EGG
◆ A SMOOTH PLATE

What's going on?
The liquid inside the raw egg has inertia and carries on swirling around inside when you grab the shell. When you let go, the whole egg starts spinning again.

Demolish the tower

Build a tower of draughts near the edge of a smooth table. Put a ruler on the table next to the tower with one end sticking out past the end of the table. Holding this end, slice the ruler quickly through the bottom of the tower by sliding it along the table with a flicking motion. With practice, you should be able to knock out the bottom draught one by one without toppling the tower.

YOU WILL NEED
10
◆ DRAUGHTS
◆ A RULER
◆ A SMOOTH TABLE

What's going on?
The quick push needed to knock the bottom draught out is too small a force to overcome the inertia of the whole tower, which stays put. The magician's trick of whipping the tablecloth out from under some plates and glasses relies on inertia in the same way.

BELT UP!
These inertia-reel seatbelts unwind easily when you pull gently to put them on. If the car stops suddenly, for example in an accident, the children's inertia will keep them moving forwards. This tugs quickly on the seatbelts, which instantly lock and hold the children safely in their seats.

MATTER AND MATERIALS

Peter Mellett

Getting started

The world we live in is made from matter. What exactly is this? Matter includes anything that has mass and takes up space. Our bodies, the air we breathe and the water we drink are all examples of matter. The different types of matter that we use to make things from are called materials.

Some materials, like rocks, soil, air, water and wood, are natural.

Other materials, like metals, glass, plastics and paper, are manufactured, or made by people.

This section of the book shows you how different sorts of matter and materials behave. It will help you understand how different materials are tested and chosen before they are used in manufacturing or building.

The right stuff

You'll need a few everyday things like string, rubber bands, a plastic bottle, and some other items you can find in the kitchen.

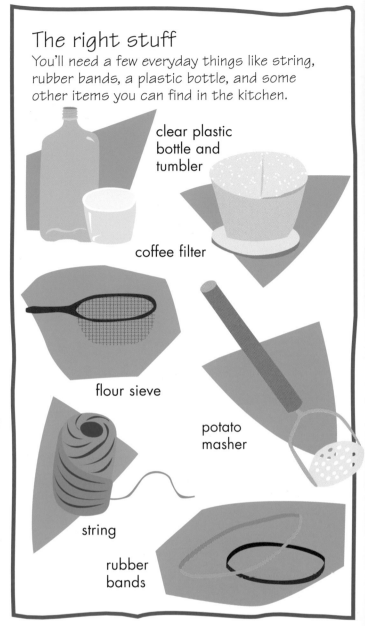

clear plastic bottle and tumbler

coffee filter

flour sieve

potato masher

string

rubber bands

Getting organised

Carry out your experiments on a firm table. But don't forget to cover it first with newspaper to protect its surface.

If you need to pour water, put a shallow tray underneath to catch any spills.

When using a hammer, first put down an old chopping board on a firm surface like a table or the floor.

Clock symbol

The clock symbol at the start of each experiment shows you approximately how many minutes the activity should take. All the experiments take between 5 and 40 minutes. If you are using glue, allow extra time for drying.

Warning

Some activities involve heat or flames, or the use of a hammer. Ask an adult for help with these, and with any other activities where you see this warning symbol.

Don't touch your face or rub your eyes, especially if you are using materials such as salt, washing soda or soil.

Always wash your hands and scrub your nails thoroughly after you have finished working.

Having problems?

Don't give up if at first you have problems with some of the activities. Even Einstein had his bad days!

If things don't seem to be working, read through each step of the activity again and then have another go.

If you get really stuck, remember that adults at home can help you with explanations. School teachers can also help if you show this book to them.

Stuck for words?

If you come across a word you don't understand, or you just want to find out a bit more, have a look in the Glossary on pages 150–157.

Denting and squeezing

Different materials have different properties – for example, the materials your clothes are made of are soft and stretchy, but materials used for building, such as concrete and brick, are hard and strong. Scientists test materials to measure and compare their properties. In this way, they can choose the best materials for making or manufacturing different things.

⚠ Hard or soft?

Trying to dent or scratch a material helps to show how hard it is. Ask an adult for permission to use the hammer, and to help you with this activity.

YOU WILL NEED
20
- A 10CM NAIL
- A HAMMER
- AN OLD SOCK
- CARDBOARD 5CM X 25CM
- A MAGNIFYING GLASS
- AN OLD KITCHEN BOARD
- SAMPLES OF SOLID MATERIALS SUCH AS WOOD, A CLAY FLOWERPOT, PLASTIC AND METAL SPOONS, A PIECE OF STONE, A RUBBER

1 Make a hole 2cm from each end of the cardboard strip. Bend the strip into a 'U' shape and push the nail through the holes, making sure it is held firmly.

3 Take the sample out of the sock. Use the magnifying glass to see whether the nail has dented or scratched the material. Now try doing steps 2 and 3 with the other sample materials and see what happens to them.

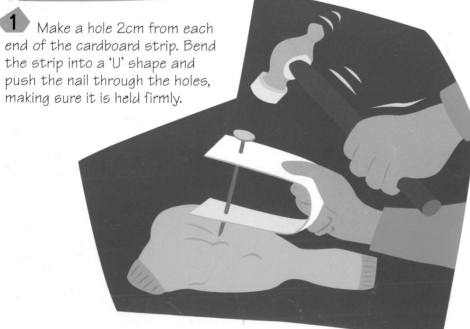

2 Put one of your samples inside the sock on top of the board. Place the point of the nail on top of the sample. Hit the head of the nail with a firm blow. The hammer should drop no more than 15cm.

What's going on?
Different materials react in different ways to being hit hard. Some, like stone and pottery, are so hard they can't be dented at all. But they are brittle and sometimes shatter. Others, like metals, are hard but not brittle. The nail will leave a small scratch in them. Materials like wood are softer, and the nail will actually make a hole in them. Plastics can be soft, hard, tough or brittle.

Squeezing materials

Place your samples on the board and squeeze them, one at a time, under the potato masher. See what happens to each material as you steadily increase the force.

What can you feel as you squeeze each material?

What's going on?

Squeezing a material tests how well it stands up to a force called compression. Elastic materials like the pieces of pencil eraser spring back when the force stops. Brittle substances like dried pasta shatter instead. Modelling clay isn't elastic like the pencil eraser. The force breaks it up so that it is squeezed through the holes of the potato masher.

FLASHBACK

The first metal

Six and a half thousand years ago, people in Egypt were the first to discover metal – in the form of copper. Like most metals, copper is found in stony materials called ores. The Egyptians blasted air into a furnace to make charcoal burn white-hot. This freed the copper so they could collect it and use it to make things with.

MATERIALS IN YOUR LIFE
How much of our world today is natural? The natural materials you are most likely to see are wood, stone, cotton and wool. Most materials are manufactured. Plastics are made from crude oil. Metals like iron, steel, copper and aluminium come from rocky ores.

Stretching and snapping

The extent to which a material can be pulled and stretched is called its tensile strength. Materials with a great tensile strength are chosen by engineers to do certain jobs. The steel cable of a crane, for example, has a high tensile strength and is able to support a very heavy load.

Threads and wires

Compare the tensile strength of three different materials. Remember to repeat the activity using a different thread each time!

1 Lie the broom flat on top of the two stools, as shown in the picture.

YOU WILL NEED
20
◆ A 2-LITRE PLASTIC BOTTLE
◆ A BROOM HANDLE
◆ TWO KITCHEN STOOLS OR CHAIRS
◆ A MEASURING JUG CONTAINING A LITRE OF WATER
◆ A MARKER PEN
◆ THREE THREADS OF THE SAME THICKNESS, EG REAL WOOL, DENTAL FLOSS (NYLON), FUSE WIRE (COPPER)

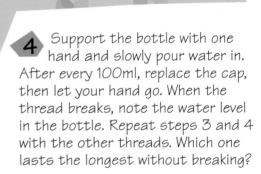

2 Pour a litre of water into the bottle. Do this slowly so you can mark the water level on the bottle for every 100ml you pour. 100ml of water has a mass of 100g, so label the marks 100g, 200g, 300g, and so on.

4 Support the bottle with one hand and slowly pour water in. After every 100ml, replace the cap, then let your hand go. When the thread breaks, note the water level in the bottle. Repeat steps 3 and 4 with the other threads. Which one lasts the longest without breaking?

3 Tip the water out. Tie the end of one thread around the neck of the bottle and the other end around the broom handle. The bottle should hang a little above the floor.

What's going on?
Gravity pulls downwards on the water in the bottle. This creates a pulling force called tension in the thread, which causes it to stretch and then snap. How quickly this happens depends on how thick the thread is and what it is made from. Wool, a natural fibre, isn't very strong. Dental floss, made from a type of plastic called nylon, and copper fuse wire both have a much greater tensile strength than wool.

Testing thin sheets

Cut out strips of each material 1cm wide by 15cm long. Wrap a strip tightly around the clothes peg and hold it firmly. Squeeze the peg harder and harder until the material breaks. Do this with each strip.

Which materials snap most easily?

YOU WILL NEED
15
- THIN SHEETS OF MATERIAL, EG A CRISP PACKET, CLINGFILM, NEWSPAPER AND A PAPER TOWEL
- A CLOTHES PEG
- A PAIR OF SCISSORS

What's going on?

Some materials are more elastic than others, which means they stretch further before they break. Paper materials are made from particles called fibres, which break apart quite easily. Plastic materials like clingfilm are made from particles called molecules. These hold strongly together, stretching before they part.

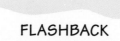

FLASHBACK

Poly bags

Polythene is made from a gas called ethene. It was invented in the UK in 1933 and was used to insulate cables in aircraft radar sets. During the 1950s, polythene replaced paper for wrapping food and for making carrier bags. Nowadays, we use poly bags like this for carrying shopping, but if you overload them, they'll eventually break!

CRANES AND CABLES

The cables of a crane are made from steel. They can support huge loads without breaking. The tensile strength of steel is four times greater than copper and ten times greater than nylon.

49

Soil

Soil is one of the most important materials in the world. Nearly all plants need soil to grow and most animals depend on plants as the source of their food. If there was no soil, there would be almost no life on the land. There are many different sorts of soil, but all of them are a mixture of sand, clay and the rotted remains of dead plants called humus.

Testing soil

Find out what your local soil is like – how much water does it absorb and how well does water drain through it?

YOU WILL NEED
- DRY SOIL
- A 500ML PLASTIC DRINKS BOTTLE
- A SPOON
- SCISSORS
- COTTON WOOL
- A TABLESPOON
- A MEASURING JUG OF WATER

20

1 Cut the bottle in half. Make two cuts down each side of the lower part of the bottle. Fold the cut parts inwards to make four tabs.

3 Add six tablespoonfuls of soil and then gently pour in 200ml of water. Time how long it takes the water to pass through the soil. Then measure the amount of water that runs out of the soil.

2 Turn the top half of the bottle upside down to make a funnel. Now push it down into the bottom half of the bottle so that the tabs grip the bottle neck. Push a ball of cotton wool into the bottle neck.

What's going on?

Water drains through soil by trickling through the spaces between the soil particles. Not all of the added water drains out because some is absorbed by the clay and humus in the soil. The sandier the soil, the more water will drain out. This is because sand does not absorb water. Clay particles are hundreds of times smaller than sand grains. They block the spaces between sand and humus and slow the downward movement of water. Water cannot pass at all through some clay soils. You can tell from the amount of water that drains through whether your soil is full of sand or clay.

What's in your soil?

Quarter fill the bottle with soil and then fill two thirds with water. Screw on the cap and shake hard. Let the bottle stand and watch the different layers form as the soil settles.

YOU WILL NEED
- A PLASTIC BOTTLE WITH CAP
- DRY SOIL
- WATER

10

humus

floating particles of clay

clay

silt

sand

gravel

What's going on?

Large grains of sand and gravel are the first to settle to the bottom. The next layer up is fine silty sand, followed by clay particles. Floating above the clay layer are tiny clay particles too small to settle to the bottom. You may also see humus floating on the surface. By testing different soil samples, you can see how soil varies from place to place.

Hardness of rocks

Rub each rock sample on the emery paper to see how easily it crumbles into powder. After rubbing, look at each surface to see how smooth or rough it is.

YOU WILL NEED
- SAMPLES OF DIFFERENT ROCKS, EG CHALK, SANDSTONE, GRANITE
- COARSE EMERY PAPER

10

How do you think sand is made in nature?

What's going on?

Emery paper is coated with very hard and abrasive (rough) particles. They cut easily into soft rock and break it down into a sandy powder. The weather has the same effect on rocks, but it takes millions of years to change large boulders into grains of sand.

SOIL POCKETS
All over the world, mountain plants grow in tiny pockets of soil hidden in cracks between the rocks. Soil contains chemicals that all plants need to grow.

Moving heat

Heat moves through solids by a process called conduction. Some materials, like metals, allow heat to pass easily. They are good conductors of heat. Other materials, like paper and plastics, do not allow heat to pass easily. They are called insulators and are poor conductors of heat. We use insulating materials to keep things warm.

Heat loss
Hot drinks cool down because heat moves from the hot liquid to the cooler air outside.

Keeping warm
Find out which insulating material keeps a hot drink hottest for the longest.

YOU WILL NEED
- FOUR CHINA MUGS
- A POLYTHENE BAG WITH TIE HANDLES
- FOUR THIN RUBBER BANDS
- NEWSPAPER
- COTTON WOOL
- HAND-HOT WATER
- A CLOCK

20

1 Wrap layers of newspaper around a mug and hold in place with a rubber band. Cover another mug with cotton wool. Place the third mug upright in an open polythene bag and leave the fourth uncovered.

2 Ask an adult to heat water until it is hand-hot (45°C). Fill each mug to the same level, 2cm from the top. Seal the polythene bag with a rubber band so it fits loosely around the mug.

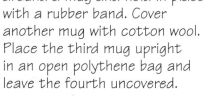

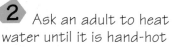

What's going on?
You should find that the water in the mug sealed inside the polythene bag has stayed the hottest, while the water in the uncovered mug is the coolest. Air is a good insulator, so long as it doesn't move around too much. The polythene bag holds a layer of air around the mug that stops heat escaping. Cotton wool contains air trapped in its fibres. Newspaper also contains air, although less than cotton wool. Most insulating materials rely on trapped air to stop heat flowing away.

3 After 15 minutes, use a finger to test the water in each mug. Arrange the four mugs in order, from the hottest down to the coolest.

Testing heat conduction

Stick a bead to the handle end of each spoon with a blob of butter or margarine. Stand the bowl on the newspaper and arrange the spoons so their handles stick out around the rim. Ask an adult to pour freshly boiled water into the bowl. Time how long it takes for the bead to drop from each spoon.

YOU WILL NEED
- BUTTER OR MARGARINE
- A METAL, PLASTIC AND WOODEN SPOON
- A HEAT-PROOF GLASS BOWL
- THREE SMALL PLASTIC BEADS
- BOILED WATER (ASK AN ADULT)
- NEWSPAPER

20

What makes the beads drop off?

What's going on?

Conduction carries heat up the handle of each spoon, which causes the butter to melt and the bead to fall off. Metal is a better conductor than wood or plastic. The end of the metal spoon becomes hot quickest and the bead drops off this spoon first. It takes longest for the bead to fall from the wooden spoon because wood contains air and is a poor conductor of heat.

Heat is a form of energy

Two hundred years ago, scientists thought that heat was an invisible fluid. But in 1851, William Thomson introduced the modern idea that heating something increases the energy of its particles and makes them move about more rapidly.

WINTER WARMTH

Have you ever wondered why birds puff themselves up in cold weather? Under their feathers are fluffy fibres that trap layers of air. These insulating layers cut down heat loss and keep the birds warm.

Solids, liquids and gases

Our world is made from millions of different materials, but all this matter exists in just three main forms – as solids, as liquids or as gases. Solids such as bricks and ice cubes are hard and have a fixed shape. Liquids such as water are runny and do not have a fixed shape. They have a flat surface and fill the bottom of a container. Gases spread out in all directions, so they are often kept in a closed container.

Feel the difference

See what happens when you try to squeeze a gas (air), a liquid (water) and a solid (ice). You'll need extra time to make the ice in step 3!

YOU WILL NEED
- AN EMPTY 500ML BOTTLE WITH A SCREW CAP
- WATER
- A LONG BALLOON
- A FREEZER

15

1 Take the empty bottle, with its cap screwed on tightly, and squeeze it in your hand. What happens to the bottle?

3 Fill a balloon with water (over a sink!) and then tie it up. Squeeze the balloon and feel how the water moves around inside. Place the balloon in a freezer for one hour. Now see if you can move the water around inside the balloon.

2 Now unscrew the cap and, over a sink, fill the bottle with water until it overflows. Screw the cap on tightly and try squeezing the bottle again. Can you still squash it easily?

What's going on?

Air is a gas and is compressible, which means it can be squeezed into a smaller space. Water is a liquid and is not compressible, which is why you can't squeeze the bottle filled with water. Liquids and gases are called fluids because they can flow from one place to another. When the temperature falls below 0°C, water freezes to make solid ice. Solids cannot flow and they are not compressible.

Gases have mass

Tie a piece of string to each end of the wooden rod. Tie the other end of each piece of string to the ring-pull on the cans. Hang the rod by its centre from underneath the stool so that the cans are evenly balanced. Ask an adult to gently pull the ring on one can to open it slightly, then let the cans hang in balance.

How does the balance change over the next half hour?

What's going on?

You'll see that the balance of the cans is disturbed and that the open can rises slightly. This is because fizzy drinks contain a gas called carbon dioxide dissolved in flavoured water. Once the can has been opened, the carbon dioxide escapes slowly from the liquid, causing the mass of the liquid to decrease. This means the contents of the open can weigh less than they did when it was closed.

FLASHBACK

John Dalton was an English chemist who lived from 1766 to 1844. He said that matter is made up from invisible particles. In solid materials, the particles are fixed together, but in liquids they can slide around past each other. The particles in gases are far apart and travel at great speed.

INFLATABLE DINGHY

Gases like air are made up from particles that are far apart. But to inflate this rescue dinghy, air has been pumped in under pressure, which squeezes the air particles closely together. This makes the dinghy firm and buoyant in the water.

Mixing materials

Most materials are not one single pure substance. They are usually made up of different substances mixed together in different ways. For example, pastry dough is a mixture of flour, fat and water, while fizzy drinks consist of water, sugar, flavourings and carbon dioxide gas. The right ingredients must be chosen to make up each different mixture.

Solutions

We can mix water with sugar or salt to make something called a solution. The solution behaves differently to ordinary water.

YOU WILL NEED
◆ WARM WATER
◆ SOLID MATERIALS SUCH AS SUGAR, SALT AND SAND
◆ FOUR CLEAR PLASTIC CUPS
◆ A TEASPOON
◆ A MAGNIFYING GLASS
◆ A FREEZER

20

Which of the grains disappear in the water?

1 Place a few grains of each solid on the table. Look at them through the magnifying glass. Can you see a difference in their shape and size? The grains of salt and sugar have straight sides — they are called crystals.

2 Half fill one of the cups with warm water. Add a pinch of sugar and watch what happens to each grain. Then add a heaped spoonful of sugar and stir the mixture. Notice how the grains dissolve and disappear.

3 Half fill another cup with water. Place this and the cup of sugary water in the freezer for two or three hours. Try to look at them every 15 minutes to see what's happening. Now repeat steps 2 and 3 with the salt, and then the sand.

What's going on?

Sugar and salt crystals dissolve (break down) when they are mixed with water. We call the result a sugar solution (or salt solution). When the crystals dissolve, they break into particles that are too small to see. These particles spread evenly through the water. Dissolved substances make freezing happen at a lower temperature than with pure liquids, so the sugar and salt solutions will take longer to freeze than the pure water. Unlike sugar and salt, sand is insoluble – it doesn't dissolve.

Investigating cake mixture

Ask an adult to help you collect all the ingredients and equipment needed to bake some small cakes. Watch how the ingredients change as you mix them together. Then see the mixture change again once it has been baked in the oven.

How do you change soggy cake mixture into cakes?

What's going on?

It's amazing how different a baked cake looks and tastes from the original raw ingredients. Cake mixture usually contains flour, eggs, sugar and fat. While it cooks in the oven, heat makes the mixture expand and changes its colour, texture and taste.

FLASHBACK

16th-century alchemist in his laboratory

Alchemists were early chemists who worked more than 400 years ago. They boiled, melted and dissolved things a bit like modern chemists do today. They believed that if they mixed the right ingredients together, they could change cheap metals into gold. They didn't understand that mixtures contain different substances arranged in a certain way.

SAWING UP CHIPBOARD
Wood is a great material for making things. But it has a disadvantage – a plank of wood can't be any wider than the tree trunk from which it is cut. So manufacturers produce chipboard – wood chippings and sawdust bonded together by glue. It comes in big sheets and is easy to cut into shape.

Expansion and contraction

When solids, liquids and gases are heated, they take in energy and their temperature gets higher. As this happens, the substance expands. It takes up more space and we say that its volume increases. As the substance gets cooler, it loses energy and its temperature decreases. This time the volume decreases and the substance contracts, or gets smaller.

Hot and cold air

This activity helps you to see how air – an invisible gas – expands and contracts when it is heated and cooled. Ask an adult to help you with the glass and the hot water.

YOU WILL NEED
◆ A SMALL, STRONG GLASS BOTTLE, EG EMPTY KETCHUP BOTTLE
◆ A DRINKING STRAW
◆ MODELLING CLAY
◆ A TEA TOWEL
◆ HOT WATER (ASK AN ADULT)
◆ A COLD, WET CLOTH
◆ A BOWL OF WATER

15

What's going on?

By heating the bottle with the warm cloth, you are heating the air inside it. Heat energy makes the tiny particles of air move around faster and they take up more space. As a result, the air expands and bubbles out of the straw. Cooling the bottle has the opposite effect. The particles slow down and take up less space. The air contracts and water enters the bottle.

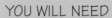

1 Gently wrap a ball of modelling clay around the straw near to one end. Push the clay firmly into the neck of the bottle to make an airtight seal.

2 Ask an adult to soak the tea towel in hot water and wrap it all around the bottle.

3 Turn the wrapped bottle upside down and dip the end of the straw under the water in the bowl. What do you notice?

4 Keep the end of the straw under the surface of the water. Unwrap the hot cloth, then wrap the cold cloth around the bottle. Now watch what happens to the water!

Heating water

Use the same equipment as before. This time, fill the bottle to the top with cold water before you fit the straw. Make sure some water rises about halfway up the straw, and mark the position with a pencil. Now stand the bottle in a bowl of hot water and watch the water level in the straw.

YOU WILL NEED

10

◆ BOTTLE, STRAW AND MODELLING CLAY AS BEFORE
◆ A BOWL OF HOT WATER (ASK AN ADULT)
◆ A PENCIL

Do liquids expand as much as gases?

What's going on?

The particles in water move more slowly than the particles in air. Liquid particles are closer together than gas particles and must slide past each other as they move. Heating water makes the particles move faster which makes the liquid expand and rise up the straw. But the effect isn't so great as the expansion of gases.

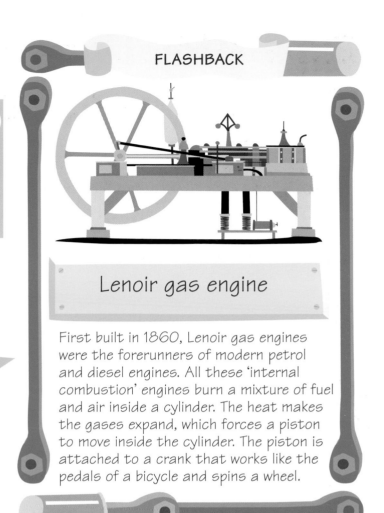

Lenoir gas engine

First built in 1860, Lenoir gas engines were the forerunners of modern petrol and diesel engines. All these 'internal combustion' engines burn a mixture of fuel and air inside a cylinder. The heat makes the gases expand, which forces a piston to move inside the cylinder. The piston is attached to a crank that works like the pedals of a bicycle and spins a wheel.

HOW THERMOMETERS WORK
When someone takes your temperature, a liquid metal (mercury) inside the thermometer responds to the heat in your mouth by expanding. As it does this, the mercury moves along a very thin tube that is marked by a temperature scale.

Heating substances

When you heat a substance, its temperature increases. This rise in temperature causes many substances to change their appearance. For example, water bubbles when it boils and bread changes into toast. When heating stops, the temperature falls again. Water stops bubbling, so we say that the change is only temporary. Toast, on the other hand, does not change back into bread when it cools. Heat here has caused a permanent change.

Gentle heating

Some substances change when the temperature rises only slightly. When you do this activity, don't touch the lamp bulb, as it will get hot.

YOU WILL NEED 20
- ◆ A BLOB OF BUTTER
- ◆ A PIECE OF CHOCOLATE
- ◆ A PIECE OF CANDLE WAX
- ◆ SUGAR
- ◆ ALUMINIUM FOIL
- ◆ SCISSORS
- ◆ AN ADJUSTABLE DESK LAMP
- ◆ A DRINKING STRAW

1 Cut out four 10cm squares of aluminium foil. Fold up the edges and pinch the corners to make four small boxes with an open top and a flat bottom.

2 Put a small amount of each substance into the aluminium boxes so that each box contains something different.

3 Ask an adult to switch on the lamp and point it straight downwards, about 5cm above the boxes. Watch for five minutes to see how heat from the lamp affects the different substances.

4 Switch off the lamp and move it away from the boxes. Now stir each of the substances with the straw to see how they have changed. Then let them cool.

What's going on?

The lamp raises the temperature to about 75°C and gently heats the four substances. Remember that water boils when we heat it to 100°C. The butter, chocolate and candle wax all become liquids when they are gently heated in this way. We say that they have melted. When they cool down again, they change back into solids. So melting is a temporary change. Sugar is not affected by the heat from an electric lamp and so does not change at all.

Stronger heating

Some substances need stronger heat to make them change. Set the oven to 200°C. Put a little sugar, salt and egg into each of the aluminium boxes and place them on a baking sheet. Ask an adult to put them in the oven and then get them out after 15 minutes. Which substances look different?

YOU WILL NEED
◆ ALUMINIUM BOXES
   (AS MADE EARLIER)
◆ SUGAR
◆ SALT
◆ RAW EGG
◆ A BAKING SHEET

15

What's going on?

Sugar melts at oven temperature and then starts to change into a brown, sticky substance called caramel. When caramel cools, it becomes solid. So it is a permanent change. Egg bakes inside an oven. This change is also permanent. This is because particles in the sugar and egg break apart and join up in a new way. Salt is not affected. It must be heated to over 850°C before it melts. When cool, it becomes solid salt again.

High-temperature heating

Place some sugar on an old teaspoon. Ask an adult to light the nightlight and hold the spoon over it for a while to heat it. What do you see?

YOU WILL NEED
◆ AN OLD TEASPOON
◆ SUGAR
◆ MATCHES (ASK AN ADULT)
◆ A NIGHTLIGHT IN A
   SAUCER OF WATER

15

What makes the sugar turn black?

What's going on?

Sugar is made up from carbon, hydrogen and oxygen. When heated to about 500°C, it breaks down into black carbon, which is what you see on the spoon, and steam, which rises. When this happens, we say the sugar decomposes. It is a permanent change.

SHAPING GLASS
Glass gradually gets softer as the temperature rises. To shape glass, workers blow down an iron pipe to make the bubbles of glass expand. They cut open the bubbles to produce beautiful jugs and ornaments.

Changing state

Matter can exist in three states – as solids, liquids or gases. When we heat a substance, it sometimes changes its state. Heat can make a solid melt to form a liquid or a liquid boil to form a gas. These changes of state are temporary because cooling reverses the changes. Gases condense into liquids and liquids freeze and become solid again.

Gas

to liquid

to solid

The air is full of invisible water vapour. You can use a freezing mixture to trap this gas and turn it into ice, which you can see.

YOU WILL NEED

30

- ICE
- A TEA TOWEL
- TWO RUBBER BANDS
- A ROLLING PIN
- SALT
- A LARGE DARK-COLOURED MUG
- A SPOON

FLASHBACK

See you later, water vapour

Over millions of years, flowing water has helped to shape the surface of the Earth. Heat from the Sun makes sea water evaporate (change into water vapour). Vapour rises into the air, cools and forms clouds of tiny water droplets. These droplets fall as rain. As rivers carry water back to the sea, they slowly carve out valleys between hills and mountains.

3 You will see that a white solid forms on the outside of the mug. It reaches up to the same level on the outside as the ice and salt inside. Scrape some of the solid into the spoon and watch it melt to form a liquid.

1 Place ten ice cubes along one edge of the tea towel and roll it into a sausage shape. Twist a rubber band around each end of the tea towel and place it on a firm surface. Now crush the ice with the rolling pin.

2 Half fill the mug with crushed ice. Add about a quarter of a mugful of salt. Stir the mixture and then leave the mug undisturbed for about 20 minutes.

Boiling and evaporation

Wet two cotton handkerchiefs and wring them out. Hang one in a warm or sunny place and the other in a cool place. Check every five minutes to see how each hanky is drying.

YOU WILL NEED
20
◆ TWO COTTON HANDKERCHIEFS
◆ A SUNNY SPOT OR A WARM PLACE INDOORS
◆ A COOL PLACE
◆ WATER

Which handkerchief dries the fastest?

What's going on?

You probably won't be surprised to see that the wet handkerchief in the warm place dries faster than the one in the cool place. But why is this? As water takes in heat from the surrounding air, it changes and becomes a gas called water vapour. When this happens, we say that the water has evaporated. The higher the temperature, the quicker the rate of evaporation. So the hanky in the warm place dries faster than the one in the cool place because the water evaporates from it more quickly.

What's going on?

The temperature of ice drops even lower when salt is added. The mixture inside the mug makes the outside extremely cold. The air around us is a gas which contains water vapour dissolved in it. When this invisible vapour touches the outside of the mug, it condenses – which means it changes into liquid water. This immediately freezes into solid ice. When you scrape some of this into the spoon, it warms up and melts to form liquid water.

LIQUID STEEL
Steel melts at around 1,540°C. When this happens, it glows white hot and is nearly eight times heavier than the same amount of water. Here liquid steel is being poured into moulds to make parts for engines.

Permanent changes

As we saw on pages 60 and 61, some changes are temporary and can be easily reversed. For example, chocolate melts when it is heated but changes back to solid chocolate when cooled. Other changes are permanent and cannot be reversed. For example, boiling an egg changes it permanently. There are three main ways of making permanent changes happen – by mixing substances together, by heating them or by passing electricity through them.

Mix for a change

Mixing vinegar and bicarbonate of soda together creates carbon dioxide gas, which puts out flames. You must ask an adult to do steps 2 and 3 of this activity.

YOU WILL NEED
- BICARBONATE OF SODA
- A HEATPROOF PUDDING BOWL
- A SHORT CANDLE
- VINEGAR
- MODELLING CLAY
- A DESSERT SPOON

15

1 Use the modelling clay to fix the candle firmly in the centre of the bowl. Place five level spoonfuls of bicarbonate of soda around the candle.

2 Ask an adult to light the candle, then to spoon vinegar down the inner side of the bowl, avoiding the flame. Watch how the liquid and powder froth as they mix.

3 Ask the adult to stop adding the vinegar when the froth is about halfway up the candle. The candle will suddenly go out. Now ask them to try to re-light it.

What's going on?
A permanent change takes place when bicarbonate of soda and vinegar are mixed together. The particles in these two substances join up in a different way to make new substances. One of the new substances is a gas called carbon dioxide, which causes the mixture to froth. This gas is heavier than air. Although you can't see it, it fills the bowl and extinguishes, or puts out, the flame. Carbon dioxide is used in many types of fire extinguisher.

Bake a model

Mould some bakeable modelling clay into a shape to make a model. Think about how it looks and feels while you do this. Then ask an adult to follow the instructions and bake your model in the oven. Let it cool. How does it look and feel now?

YOU WILL NEED 15
◆ BAKEABLE MODELLING CLAY
◆ AN OVEN

What changes happen when you bake the clay?

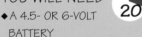

What's going on?

Modelling clay is soft and easy to squeeze. It contains long, thin particles that slide past each other when you squeeze the clay. But once the clay has been baked in the oven, permanent links form between the particles. They can no longer slide around, and this is why your baked model is now hard.

Electric effect

Get an adult to strip the ends of the wires. Ask them to connect one end of each wire to the battery and dip the other end into some salty water. Watch what happens to the wires. Do you recognise the smell?

YOU WILL NEED 20
◆ A 4.5- OR 6-VOLT BATTERY
◆ TWO INSULATED WIRES 20CM LONG
◆ SALT
◆ A CLEAR PLASTIC CUP OF WATER

What's going on?

Electricity changes part of the salt solution into a gas, which makes bubbles. This gas is called chlorine. You can smell it in swimming pools, where it is used to disinfect the water.

A CHEMICAL REACTION

These children are studying chemical reactions that make materials change permanently. The substances they start with are called reactants. After the reactants change, they make new substances called products.

Burning

The scientific name for burning is combustion. To make burning happen, you need fuel and air. Fuels can be solid, like wood and coal, or liquid, like petrol and paraffin oil. When a fuel burns, it mixes with oxygen in the air and a permanent change takes place, which gives out heat. Before they can burn quickly, solid and liquid fuels must change into gases. When they burn, many common fuels produce carbon dioxide gas and water vapour.

⚠ Air and fire

Find out how flames need air to burn, and see how they use up just a part of it. Ask an adult to do this activity for you to watch.

YOU WILL NEED   20
- A CANDLE (5CM TALL)
- A METAL ROASTING TRAY
- A TALL GLASS JAR
- WATER
- MODELLING CLAY

1 Use modelling clay to stick the candle upright in the centre of the tray. Pour water into the tray until it is about 2cm deep.

3 Watch the candle flame carefully as soon as the jar is in place. What happens to the level of the water inside the jar?

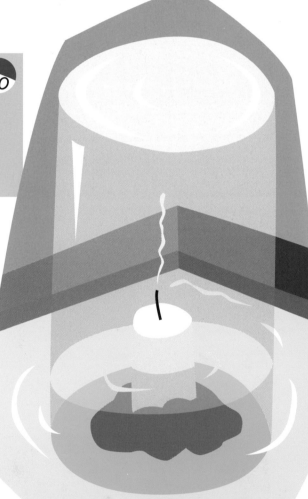

2 Ask an adult to light the candle and then to place the glass jar over it. The rim of the jar must be under the water, resting on the bottom of the tray.

What's going on?
You'll see the water level rise inside the jar. It does this to replace the oxygen that was used up by the burning flame. Once the oxygen is used up, the flame goes out. There is still air left in the jar, but now it is mostly made up of a gas called nitrogen. Fuels cannot burn when only nitrogen is present.

Drilling for oil

Cars, lorries, ships and planes use liquid fuels made from petroleum (also called crude oil). This dark, oily liquid comes from deep under the ground. The first oil well was drilled by Edwin L. Drake in 1859 at Titusville, Pennsylvania. He struck oil at a depth of just 23 metres. Modern oil wells are up to 5,000 metres deep.

FIGHTING FIRE WITH FOAM
Firefighters spray foam on to burning aircraft fuel. The foam smothers the fire and cools the burning fuel. Foam bubbles contain carbon dioxide gas and other chemicals. These prevent oxygen from helping fuel to burn.

A closer look at a flame

Ask an adult to light the candle. Look carefully, but not too closely, to see the three parts of the flame.

YOU WILL NEED
◆ A CANDLE (5CM TALL)

5

Why are there different colours?

What's going on?
The heat from the flame melts wax near the base of the wick. This melted wax soaks up the wick and into the flame. Wax on the burned part of the wick is turned by heat into a gas. This wax vapour mixes with air and burns – giving a blue part to the flame. The mixture then rises into the middle of the flame, where particles of carbon from the wax glow and give out yellow light.

Sieving solids

We can sometimes separate mixtures by using a sieve. This only works when the mixture contains solids of different sizes. For example, we can sieve soil because it is a mixture of solids such as sand, clay and humus. The larger particles stay in the sieve while the smaller ones fall through the holes and collect underneath.

Separating soil

Use two types of sieve to sort soil into four piles of different-sized particles.

YOU WILL NEED

25

- A COLANDER
- A KITCHEN SIEVE
- FOUR LARGE PIECES OF PAPER
- STERILIZED COMPOST FROM A GARDEN CENTRE
- A MAGNIFYING GLASS

FLASHBACK

Sieving flour

Flour was once made by grinding wheat between two large revolving stones. About 120 years ago, millers in Hungary and Switzerland began to use cylinder-shaped rollers to powder the grain. Ten sieves with different size holes were stacked one above the other. They separated the milled grain into different grades of flour.

3 Gently spread out some of each pile on the sheets. Look carefully through the magnifying glass to compare the particle sizes in each of the piles.

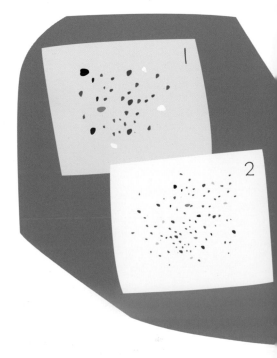

1 Number the sheets of paper 1, 2, 3 and 4. Put some compost into the colander. Hold the colander over sheet 2 and shake gently. When no more soil passes through, tip what's left in the colander on to sheet 1.

2 Take some of the particles from sheet 2 and put them into the kitchen sieve. Tap the sieve over sheet 4 until no more particles pass through. Tip what's left in the sieve on to sheet 3.

Even smaller holes

Put some soil into the tumbler. Use the rubber band to fasten the foil over the rim of the tumbler, then prick some tiny holes in the foil with the needle. Turn the tumbler upside down and then gently shake it. Look carefully at the particles that fall on to the paper.

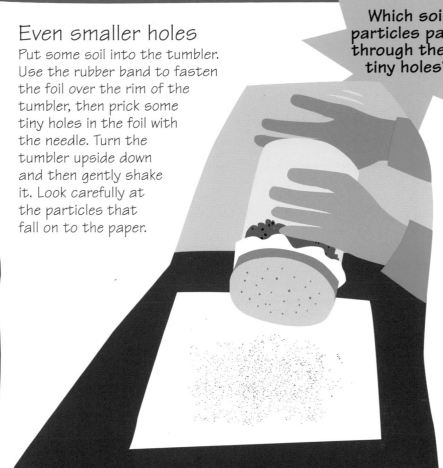

YOU WILL NEED
- WHITE PAPER
- A CLEAR PLASTIC TUMBLER
- DRY SOIL
- ALUMINIUM FOIL
- A RUBBER BAND
- A VERY FINE NEEDLE

15

What's going on?

The holes in the foil are much less than 1mm across. Clay particles are usually the only part of soil small enough to pass through. These particles appear as a dusty mark on the paper. You would need a powerful microscope to see a single clay particle.

What's going on?

The holes in a colander are about 4mm across. Only particles that are smaller than 4mm pass through the colander. The sieve separates the particles that are smaller than 4mm. It has holes about 1mm across. The particles that stay in the sieve are larger than 1mm but smaller than 4mm. The ones that go through are smaller than 1mm. Sheet 1 holds the largest particles and sheet 4 the smallest.

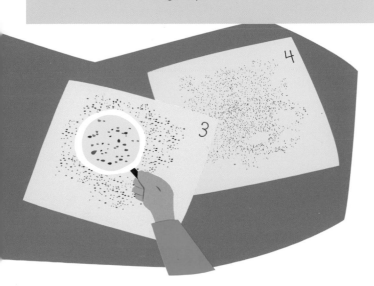

BREATHING CLEAN AIR

Wood dust from a sanding machine can harm your lungs. These men are wearing safety masks made from paper or cotton fibres. The masks work like a very fine sieve. Gaps between the fibres are large enough to allow air to pass freely, and small enough to stop wood particles from entering the mask.

Solutions and suspensions

Substances such as salt and sugar dissolve, or break down, in water. We say that they are soluble. When mixed with water, soluble substances slowly disappear as they dissolve to form a solution. Substances such as chalk and sand do not dissolve in water. We say that they are insoluble. Shaking an insoluble substance with water scatters the particles through the water and forms a mixture called a suspension.

Solution or suspension?

Add different solids to water and decide which dissolve to form a solution and which scatter to make a suspension.

1 Put one spoonful of sugar into one of the bottles. Use the plastic funnel to guide the crystals into the bottle. Add the sugar slowly so that it does not block the neck of the funnel.

3 Look carefully at each bottle to see if you can still see solid particles. Decide which solids form a solution and which solids form a suspension.

2 Repeat step 1, placing each of the other solids in its own bottle. Now half fill each bottle with water and screw on the cap. Shake each bottle ten times.

What's going on?

Sugar and coffee granules dissolve in water to make a solution. All solutions are clear and you can see right through them. A sugar solution is colourless and a coffee solution is brown. Sand and flour do not dissolve. Shaking them with water creates a suspension. Larger grains quickly settle to the bottom. Suspensions are not clear and you cannot easily see through them.

Investigating milk

Is milk a solution or a suspension? Find out by adding just one or two drops of milk to a glass of water. Look closely as the milk falls through the water.

YOU WILL NEED
- A TALL, CLEAR PLASTIC TUMBLER OF WATER
- MILK
- A TEASPOON

5

Is milk a single substance or a mixture?

What's going on?

You cannot see clearly through milk, even when you add it to water. Milk consists of droplets of fat suspended in water. Fat is insoluble in water and the droplets are too small for them to settle. Scientists call mixtures like milk 'emulsions'. This name is also given to emulsion paint, which consists of microscopic coloured droplets of oil suspended in water.

Creating colours

Paint is coloured because it contains tiny coloured particles called pigment. These particles are suspended in a liquid called the binder that sets hard when exposed to the air. Early artists ground up coloured minerals or chemicals to make pigments.

To bind the colour, they used egg white or sticky oils made from boiled tree sap.

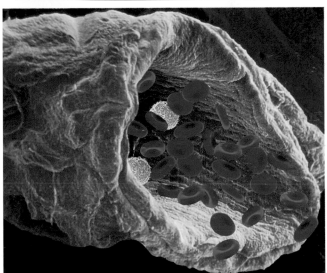

A MIX OF MIXTURES
Blood is both a solution and a suspension. It flows around your body in tubes called veins and arteries. Solid red and white blood cells are suspended in a clear liquid called plasma. This liquid is a solution of hundreds of different substances dissolved in water.

Filtering mixtures

Muddy water is an example of a suspension. It consists of tiny solid particles scattered through a liquid. To separate the particles from the suspension, you can use a filter. Filters work like sieves, but they have microscopic holes called pores, and are often made from thick, fluffy paper. The liquid part of a suspension passes through the holes between the paper fibres, while the solid particles are trapped.

Filtering flour

Mixing flour with water makes a cloudy suspension. Coffee filter paper makes the water clear again.

YOU WILL NEED
◆ A COFFEE FILTER FUNNEL
◆ COFFEE FILTER PAPER
◆ WATER
◆ PLAIN FLOUR
◆ THREE CLEAR PLASTIC TUMBLERS
◆ A TEASPOON

20

Which tumbler has the clearest liquid?

1 Add half a teaspoonful of flour to one of the tumblers. Fill the tumbler with water and stir the mixture to make a suspension of flour in water.

2 Place the funnel inside an empty tumbler and put a filter paper inside the funnel. Pour two thirds of the flour and water mixture into the filter.

3 When the tumbler is about a third full, move the funnel and the filter on to the last empty tumbler. Look inside the filter paper when all the liquid has run through. Now look at the liquid in each tumbler and notice the difference.

What's going on?

At first, liquid runs quickly through the filter. Most solid particles are trapped, but some small particles pass through. As a result, the filtered liquid in the first tumbler is slightly hazy. Liquid then passes slowly as the filter pores get blocked. Now even very small particles cannot pass, so the filtered liquid in the third tumbler is almost clear.

Filtering through sand

Cut the bottle in half. Place the funnelled end facing downwards into the base of the bottle. Fill the bottle with cotton wool, pebbles, gravel and sand, as shown, to make your filter. Pour compost mixed with water into the bottle and watch it drip through. What colour are the drips? How fast is the water passing through?

YOU WILL NEED

15

- A 500ML PLASTIC DRINKS BOTTLE
- SCISSORS
- COTTON WOOL
- SAND, GRAVEL, PEBBLES
- POTTING COMPOST
- WATER

How can filters make our tap water clean?

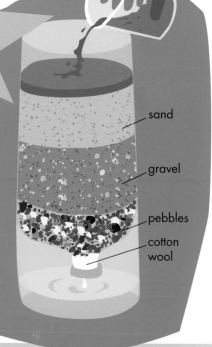

- sand
- gravel
- pebbles
- cotton wool

What's going on?

The pebbles, gravel and sand and the fibres in the cotton wool act together as a filter. They prevent the solids in the water from passing through. The trapped solids are called the residue and the liquid that passes through is called the filtrate. The tap water we drink often comes from rivers and lakes. It passes through huge sand filters that make the water clear and pure. Added chemicals kill germs.

Filtering germs

In about 1880, doctors discovered that many diseases are caused by germs. They separated germs into two sorts — 'filterable' and 'non-filterable'. 'Filterable' germs called bacteria cause illnesses such as food poisoning. They are large enough to be trapped by a filter. 'Non-filterable' germs are much smaller and pass through a filter. They are called viruses and they cause diseases like chickenpox and flu.

FEEDING THROUGH FILTERS

The humpback whale is a filter feeder. It has hundreds of thin plates called baleen in its mouth. The inside edges of the plates have brushlike fibres, which filter out food particles from the water. Every time the whale scoops about 4,000 litres of water into its mouth, it filters 20kg of tiny food particles.

73

Evaporating solutions

You can make a solution by dissolving a solid such as salt in water. The solution looks like pure water because the solid has broken down into tiny invisible particles. To make the solid reappear, you can cause the solution to evaporate, or turn into a gas. As the liquid disappears, the solid reappears because there is not enough liquid to dissolve it.

Evaporating salt solution

Solid salt seems to disappear when it dissolves in water. You can evaporate the water to get the solid salt back again.

YOU WILL NEED
- SALT
- WARM WATER
- A SAUCER
- A CLEAR PLASTIC TUMBLER
- A TEASPOON

20

What makes water evaporate?

1 Pour warm water into the tumbler until it is one third full. Add a spoonful of salt and stir until all the salt has dissolved.

2 Pour the salt solution into the saucer until there is a shallow pool, then put the saucer on a sunny windowsill or in some other warm, airy place.

3 Check the saucer twice a day for the next two or three days. What do you notice appearing on the saucer as the water gradually disappears?

What's going on?
Heat causes the water to evaporate – it changes into an invisible gas called water vapour, which escapes into the air. As the liquid slowly evaporates from the solution into the air, the dissolved salt stays behind. You will see a crusty layer of solid salt left on the saucer once all the water has evaporated.

Stalactite on a string

Fill each jar up to three quarters with hot water, then stir in sugar until no more dissolves. Fix a paperclip to each end of the wool. Drop each end into a jar so the wool hangs down between the jars. Place a saucer between the jars and leave them in a warm place. Inspect the string every day for about a week.

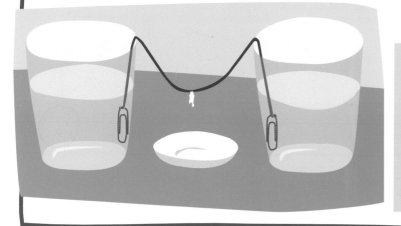

What's going on?

The solution in each jar is saturated – it is as full as it can be of dissolved sugar. The liquid soaks along the wool and collects at the lowest point between the jars. Water evaporates here, so the solid cannot remain dissolved. Solid sugar crystals form and grow bigger as the wool soaks up more solution from the jars.

FLASHBACK

Sea salt

The sea contains many dissolved substances, especially the salt that we use in our food. For thousands of years, people have used heat from the Sun to make solid salt by evaporating sea water. The Latin word for salt is 'sal', which is the origin of the word 'salary'. Roman soldiers were given salt as part of their wages.

STALACTITES AND STALAGMITES
Rainwater often trickles through underground cracks, dissolving the limestone rock underneath. As the water drips from the roof of a cave, it evaporates to leave deposits of solid limestone. Over thousands of years, they grows downwards to become stalactites. Where the drips land, stalagmites grow up from the floor.

Saturated solutions

How much sugar can you dissolve in a cup of coffee? The answer is about 20 spoonfuls. If you add any more, solid sugar stays undissolved in the bottom of the cup. When a solution cannot dissolve any more solid, it is called a saturated solution. The amount of solid needed to make a saturated solution varies from one substance to another.

How much solid?

The solubility of a substance is the amount needed to make a saturated solution. Different substances have different solubilities.

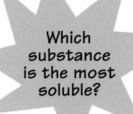

Which substance is the most soluble?

YOU WILL NEED
- BICARBONATE OF SODA
- SALT
- SUGAR
- SIX TEASPOONS
- THREE CLEAR PLASTIC TUMBLERS
- WATER
- STICKY LABELS AND PEN

25

1 Label each of the tumblers 'sugar', 'salt' etc. Half fill them with water and place a teaspoon in each.

3 Add more solid to each tumbler until no more will dissolve. Count how many spoonfuls of solid dissolve in each tumbler.

2 Add a teaspoonful of sugar to the tumbler labelled 'sugar'. Stir until the solid has dissolved. Now repeat this step in the other tumblers using bicarbonate of soda and salt.

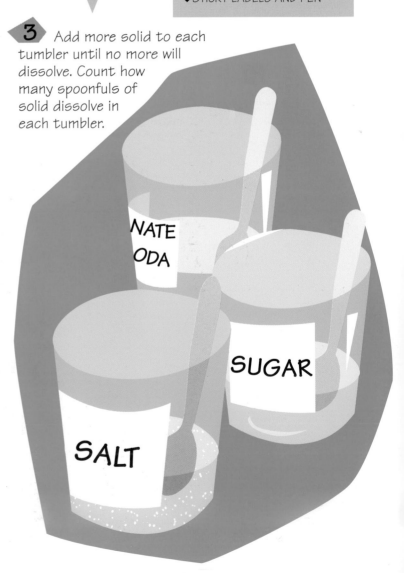

What's going on?

The tumblers each contain the same amount of water to make sure the test is fair. More sugar dissolves than salt, so you can say that sugar is more soluble than salt. Less bicarbonate of soda dissolves than sugar or salt, so it is the least soluble of the three substances.

Growing crystals

Half fill a tumbler with warm water. Stir in sugar until no more will dissolve, then pour the clear solution into the other tumbler, leaving any undisolved sugar behind. Use the pencil and cotton to suspend the paperclip in the solution. Look at the paperclip every day for about a week and see what happens.

Where do most of the crystals grow?

What's going on?

The water slowly evaporates and crystals appear when there is not enough water to dissolve all the solid. Crystals grow on places that aren't smooth, so you'll see them first on the edges of the paperclip. The water in the tumbler disappears slowly because there is only a small surface area from which it can evaporate. This slow evaporation helps large crystals to grow.

Fizzing bubbles

Place one bottle of fizzy drink in the fridge and the other in the bucket of warm water. Half an hour later, open both the bottles (over the sink!) What do you see?

Which drink – cool or warm – froths the most?

What's going on?

Fizzy drinks consist of carbon dioxide gas dissolved in flavoured water. You will see more of this gas froth out from the warm drink than from the cold drink. This is because more gas can be dissolved in cold liquids than in warm liquids. As you open the bottle, the pressure inside is released, which allows gas to bubble out of the solution and escape.

SUGAR SEEDS

Sugar is made from the juice of sugar cane and sugar beet. One hundred grams of tiny seed crystals are added to a huge tank filled with a saturated solution of sugary syrup. It takes only two hours for each seed to grow until the tank contains 20 tonnes of solid sugar crystals.

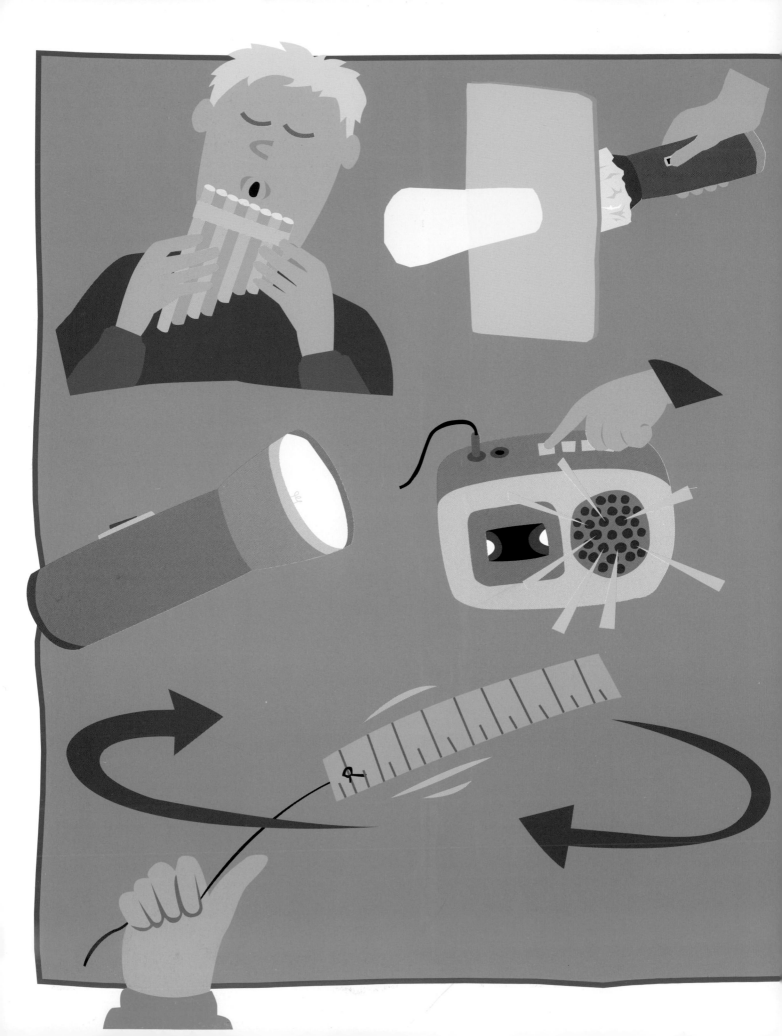

SOUND AND LIGHT

Jack Challoner

Getting started

Sound and light allow people to enjoy and understand the world around them. But have you ever wondered what sound and light actually are? In this section of the book you can find out. It is packed with activities you can try at home or at school, which will help you to understand sound and light and to realise how important they are to our lives.

See hear

The buzzing of a bumble bee, the blast of a trumpet, the roar of a jet engine, the crack of a whip – all of these are sounds. But just what is sound – how does it reach people's ears, and how do people hear?

A flash of lightning, the glare of the Sun, the glint of a diamond, the green glow of a traffic light – all of these are light. But what is light – how does it reach people's eyes, and how do people see?

What you need

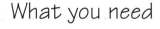

None of the activities in this section requires special scientific equipment. Most of them can be carried out using things you can find at home, like mirrors, batteries and balloons.

One thing you need in many of the activities is a torch. Make sure that your torch's batteries are not flat – the brighter the torch, the better.

You will need eyes and ears, too. If you cannot hear or see, work with someone who can.

Clock symbol

The clock symbol at the start of each experiment shows you approximately how many minutes the activity should take. All the experiments take between 5 and 30 minutes. If you are using glue allow extra time for drying.

Warning

Whenever you are experimenting, it is important to be safe.

Bright lights can be harmful to eyes. Never look directly at the Sun, especially through any telescope or binoculars – you risk being blinded for life.

Be careful when using an electric lamp of any kind. The bulb in this can get very hot and cause a burn or set something touching it alight.

Sound can be harmful, too. Try to avoid very loud sounds, especially for long periods of time – for example, try not to listen to music too loudly through earphones or headphones.

Having problems?

Some of the activities in this section can be a bit fiddly, and require patience and sometimes an extra pair of hands.

If something doesn't seem to be working, read through each step of the activity again and have another go. If there is something you don't quite understand, read the explanation again, or ask an adult to help you.

Do try all the activities – the more you explore what light and sound can do, the better you will understand them. And don't be scared to try your own versions of the activities as long as they are safe (ask an adult for advice). After all, trying something new is what scientists are best at! You may find out something new.

Stuck for words?

If you see a word you don't recognise or you want to find out more, take a look in the Glossary on pages 150–157.

Sources of sound

Take a moment to stop and listen to the sounds around you. Close your eyes if it makes it easier. Things that produce sound are called sound sources. Most sources of sound are objects moving quickly backwards and forwards, or 'vibrating'. The vibrations that produce sound are far too fast to see, but you can often feel them.

Shock wave!

Some sounds are produced by shock waves, not vibrations. A shock wave is caused by something moving very fast, like a bullet or a supersonic aeroplane. You can make a loud shock wave, using a home-made paper banger.

YOU WILL NEED
◆ ONE PIECE OF A3 PAPER
10

1 Look at the sequence of pictures that show you how to make the banger. You should begin by folding the paper lengthways. The dotted line shows you where to fold the paper.

A

B

C

D

E

F

2 Once you have made your banger, grasp it as shown between a finger and thumb. Hold the banger above your head and bring it down swiftly, as if you are hammering in a nail. As you stop, the paper fold flies out, causing a loud bang.

What's going on?
As the folded centre of the banger flies out at speed, it pushes air in front of it, creating a shock wave. The shock wave is heard as a loud bang.

Make a bull-roarer

Thread one end of the string through the hole in the ruler, and tie it securely. Use at least two firm knots. Go outside, away from other people, and hold the string, near the free end. Now, whirl the ruler around your head. You should hear a strange sound.

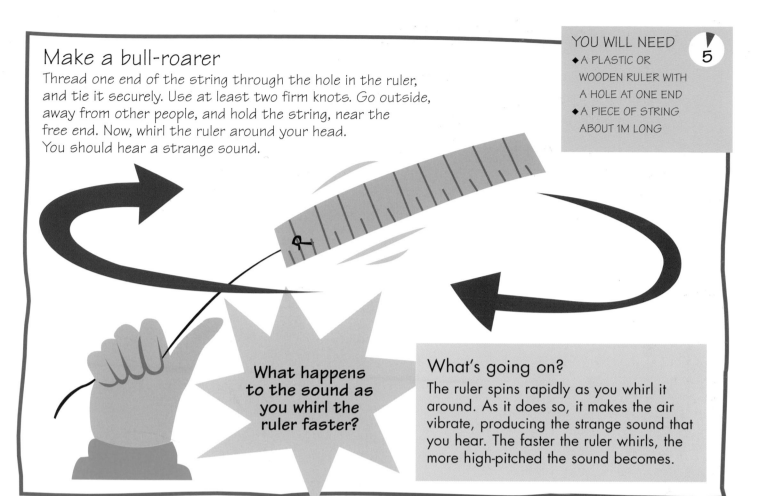

What happens to the sound as you whirl the ruler faster?

What's going on?
The ruler spins rapidly as you whirl it around. As it does so, it makes the air vibrate, producing the strange sound that you hear. The faster the ruler whirls, the more high-pitched the sound becomes.

Feel the vibrations

Gently touch both sides of your throat as you sing or shout. What do you feel? Your voice can also make a plastic bottle vibrate. Sing into an empty bottle, and feel the vibrations in the side of the bottle.

A LOUD BANG
Explosives are often used to help demolish old or unsafe buildings. The gases produced by an explosion expand rapidly, causing a shock wave. The bigger an explosion, the greater the shock wave, and the louder the sound.

Sources of light

Things that produce light, such as the Sun or a torch, are called light sources. The Sun and the torch bulb produce light because they are hot. This is called incandescence. Some light sources, such as fireflies and television screens, are not hot. They give out light by luminescence.

White hot!

Hot objects give out red light. If they get hotter still, they give out yellow. Really hot things glow white.

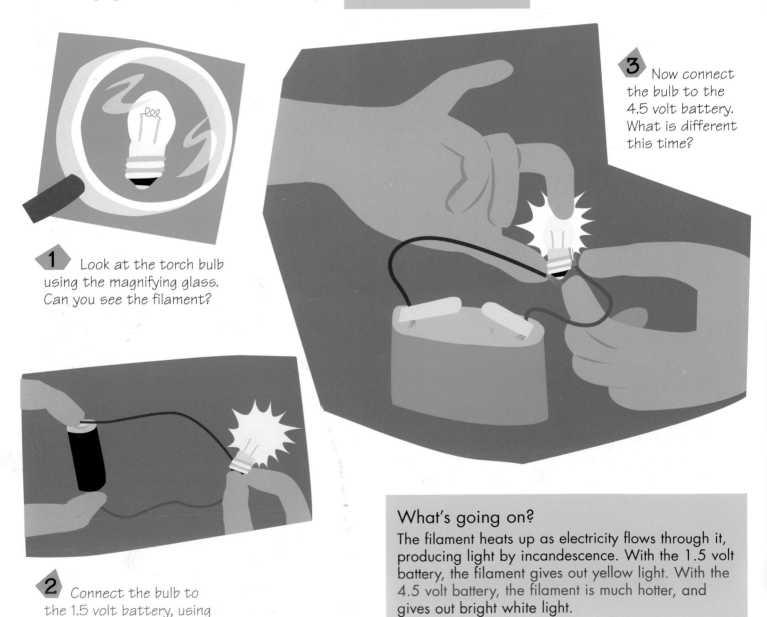

3 Now connect the bulb to the 4.5 volt battery. What is different this time?

1 Look at the torch bulb using the magnifying glass. Can you see the filament?

2 Connect the bulb to the 1.5 volt battery, using wires as shown.

What's going on?

The filament heats up as electricity flows through it, producing light by incandescence. With the 1.5 volt battery, the filament gives out yellow light. With the 4.5 volt battery, the filament is much hotter, and gives out bright white light.

Sweet light

YOU WILL NEED 5
- SUGAR CUBES
- A ROLLING PIN
- A CLEAR PLASTIC BAG

Place a few sugar cubes in the plastic bag. Find a very dark room. Stay there for at least five minutes, to make your eyes more sensitive. Now, crush the sugar cubes using the rolling pin.

What's going on?

There are many types of luminescence. One of them is triboluminescence, in which some materials give out light when they break. Sugar cubes are triboluminescent. When the sugar is crushed, the atoms break apart and give out blue light.

Can you see tiny flashes of blue light?

After glow

Make the room dark, and turn the television off. Hold the torch against the television screen. Turn on the torch for about a minute, then turn it off.

YOU WILL NEED 5
- A TORCH
- A TELEVISION

When you move the torch away from the screen what do you see?

What's going on?

A television screen is a light source. The inside of the screen is coated with dyes that can glow by luminescence. The energy of the torch light is stored in the dyes in the screen. They give out the energy gradually, producing a faint glow over a few minutes.

LIGHTS IN THE SKY
Fireworks make an impressive light display in the sky. The red, yellow and white flashes are produced by incandescence, while the bright colours are produced by luminescence.

Sound travels

The vibrations that cause sound travel in all directions as waves. If you shouted to someone standing 340 metres away from you, the sound of your voice would take about one second to reach the other person. Most of the sound we hear travels through the air, but sound can also travel through solids and liquids.

 Air waves

YOU WILL NEED
- A JUG
- WATER
- A SHALLOW TRAY
- TWO PENCILS

▶ 10

Sound waves spread out in all directions, just like water waves. This is why a sound becomes quieter the farther you are from it. A megaphone prevents sound from becoming too spread out.

3 Place the pencils into the water, as shown. Make waves again, where the pencils are close together. What happens to the waves now?

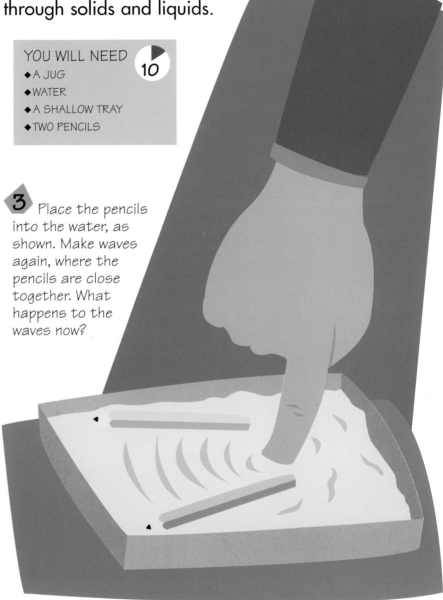

1 Put some water into the tray. Wait for it to settle.

2 Touch your finger on the water's surface. Vibrate your finger up and down to produce water waves that travel in every direction, just like sound waves through the air.

What's going on?
The more spread out a sound wave is, the quieter the sound. The pencils in the water do not allow the water waves to spread out so much. In the same way, the sides of a megaphone do not allow the sound waves to become so spread out either.

String sounds

Tie about 40cm of thread to the spoon, near the middle. Wrap the free end of the thread around a finger, and swing the spoon so that it hits against the table. Now, do the same again, but this time put the finger with the thread wrapped around it into your ear.

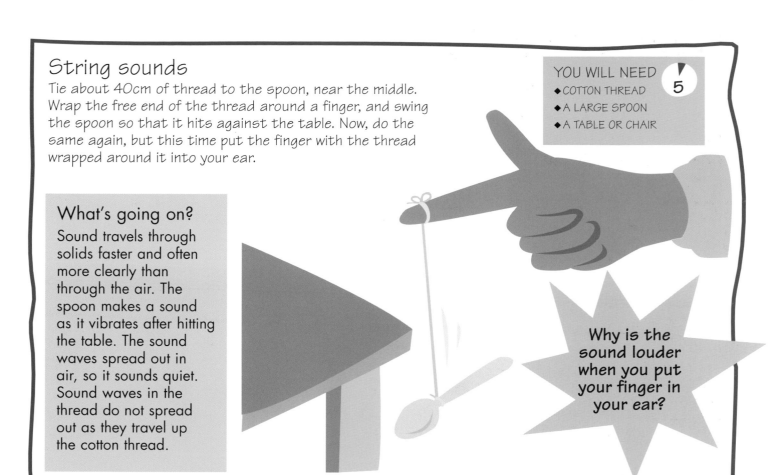

What's going on?

Sound travels through solids faster and often more clearly than through the air. The spoon makes a sound as it vibrates after hitting the table. The sound waves spread out in air, so it sounds quiet. Sound waves in the thread do not spread out as they travel up the cotton thread.

Why is the sound louder when you put your finger in your ear?

FLASHBACK

A sound idea

Probably the first person to realise that sound travels as waves was the Roman architect Vitruvius. Nearly 2,000 years ago, he wrote that sound moves like the 'waves which appear when a stone is thrown into smooth water'.

SHOUT AS LOUDLY AS YOU LIKE...
In outer space, there is no air. So, however loudly you shout, you will not be heard. Space is absolutely silent.

Light travels

When you turn on a torch, the bulb seems to light up immediately. Actually, it takes a short time for the torch light to travel to your eyes – less than a hundred millionth of a second! Even though it travels at such an incredible speed, light from the Sun takes eight minutes to reach us on Earth. Light does not travel through all materials. Where an object stops the passage of light, a shadow may form.

Seeing the light

You can only see light when it shines into your eyes! To do all these steps together, try this experiment when it is dark outside.

YOU WILL NEED
◆ A TORCH
◆ SOME NEWSPAPER
◆ TALCUM POWDER
◆ A FRIEND

5

Where is the beam of light going?

1 Put some newspaper down in a room to protect the floor, and make the room dark.

2 Ask a friend to shine the torch from one side of the room to the other, so that the torch beam passes in front of your eyes. You cannot see the beam.

3 Sprinkle the talcum powder in the path of the light beam. Suddenly, you can see where the light is going. What happens if your friend blocks part of the beam with a finger?

What's going on?

When light from the torch hits the tiny particles of talcum powder, it bounces off in all directions. Some of the light makes it into your eyes, so you can see the path of the beam. When the air is clear, and there is nothing to bounce the light into your eyes, the beam of light goes past you without you seeing it.

88

Passing through

Ask a friend to shine a torch in your direction, but not directly into your eyes. What happens if he or she holds different materials in front of the torch? Try clear plastic, tracing paper, wood, metal, and a hand.

Does light pass through some materials better than others?

What's going on?

Materials through which you can see clearly, through which light passes, are called transparent. Materials like tracing paper, which let light through, but that you cannot see through clearly, are called translucent. Opaque objects let no light through at all.

The Speed of Light

FLASHBACK

The first person to attempt to measure the speed of light was the Italian scientist Galileo Galilei. Nearly 400 years ago, one dark night, Galileo and his assistant stood far apart and flashed lanterns at each other. They tried to work out how long light from the lanterns took to pass between them. The only thing Galileo could say about light after the experiment was that it travels very fast!

4 Take the torch outside when it is dark. Shine it straight up into the air. Only if it is misty or foggy will you will be able to see the torch beam.

THE SUN THROUGH THE TREES

You can see the path of light from the Sun through the trees because of the mist. The light is bouncing off tiny droplets of water hanging in the air. The light travels in straight lines.

Different tones of sound

The sound of your voice is produced by small flaps of skin, called vocal cords, inside your throat. When you sing or speak in a high voice, as when female opera singers sing, your vocal cords vibrate very quickly. When you make a low-pitched sound, like male opera singers do, your vocal cords vibrate more slowly. All sounds may be high- or low-pitched, depending on how rapid the vibrations are that cause them.

Low and high

Low-pitched sounds are produced by slow vibrations and high-pitched sounds by more rapid vibrations. Listen carefully for the different high- and low-pitched sounds caused by the following sources of sound. Ask permission to use the hi-fi!

YOU WILL NEED
◆ A PLASTIC DRINKS BOTTLE
◆ A JUG OF WATER

5

What's going on?
The column of air inside the bottle vibrates when you blow across the top of the bottle. The shorter the air column, the faster the air vibrates, so the higher the note.

1 Fill the plastic bottle with some of the water from the jug.

2 Blow across the top of the bottle to make a note.

3 Put more water from the jug into the bottle. Blow across the top of the bottle again. How has the note changed?

High-pitched hiss

Make sure that there is no cassette in the tape recorder. Press 'PLAY', turn the volume up quite high, and stand two or three metres away from the loudspeakers. What do you hear? Now, cup your hands behind your ears while you listen to the hissing sound made by the tape recorder.

YOU WILL NEED
◆ A TAPE RECORDER HI-FI WITH LOUDSPEAKERS AND TONE CONTROLS ('BASS' AND 'TREBLE' OR JUST 'TONE')

5

Can you hear a hiss?

What's going on?
When you play a tape recorder, you can sometimes hear a hissing noise. This is a very high-pitched sound, caused by rapid vibrations in the loudspeaker. Turning down the tape recorder's 'treble' or 'tone' control removes some of the high-pitched hissing noise.

A vibrating ruler

Place a ruler on a table, so that some of the ruler hangs out over the table's edge. Press down hard on the ruler right at the edge, and 'twang' the ruler so that it makes a sound. You can see it vibrating.

YOU WILL NEED
◆ A PLASTIC RULER
◆ A TABLE

5

How can you make the sound higher or lower in pitch?

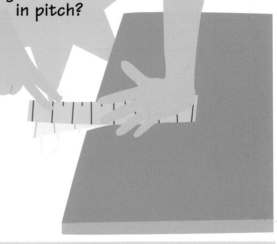

What's going on?
The longer you make the vibrating part of the ruler, the slower it vibrates, and the lower the pitch of the sound.

ON THE ALERT
Very high-pitched sounds (ultrasound) cannot be heard by human beings at all, but can be heard by some animals. This dog's ears are pricked up to hear sounds its owner may not even notice. If the animal hears anything to suggest danger, it will bark loudly as a warning.

Musical sounds

Music is sound that has a pleasing mixture of different vibrations. Musical notes have particular frequencies of vibration. Musical instruments are divided into three types, depending upon how the sound is produced. There are percussion instruments, such as drums and cymbals, that produce sound when they are hit. Wind instruments, such as trombones or clarinets, produce sound when the air inside them vibrates. Finally, string instruments, such as violins and guitars, have strings that produce sound when they are bowed or plucked.

Rubber band guitar

Make your own guitar, using rubber bands, some wood and a shoe box.

YOU WILL NEED 20
- AN EMPTY SHOE BOX
- LARGE RUBBER BANDS
- SCISSORS
- GLUE
- TWO PIECES OF WOOD, ABOUT 1CM SQUARE AND AS WIDE AS THE SHOE BOX

1 Remove the lid from the shoe box, and cut a hole in the top.

2 Using the glue, stick one piece of wood to each end of your shoe box, on either side of the hole you have cut out. Leave to dry.

3 Stretch the rubber bands across the top of the shoe box and the pieces of wood. Leave a gap of about 1cm between each rubber band. Press one finger on the rubber band at different distances while you pluck with your other hand, to play different notes.

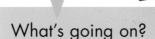

How can you make different notes on your rubber band guitar?

What's going on?

When you pluck the rubber bands, they vibrate and make a sound. The whole box vibrates, which makes the sound louder. You can raise the pitch of the note in three ways – a rubber band will produce a higher note the more stretched it is, the shorter it is, and the thinner it is.

Pan pipes

Ask an adult to help you cut the piping into eight different lengths, between 7cm and 16cm. Make eight balls of modelling clay, each about 2cm in diameter, and press each piece over one end of each of the lengths of pipe, to make a seal. Lay the pipes next to each other, so that the open ends are level with each other, from longest to shortest. Tape the pipes together. Hold the open end of one of the pan pipes against your bottom lip and gently blow air across it.

YOU WILL NEED **20**
◆ A LENGTH OF PLASTIC PIPING, ABOUT 1M LONG
◆ SCISSORS
◆ MODELLING CLAY
◆ STICKY TAPE

Which pipes produce the highest notes?

What's going on?

When you blow air across the pipes, air vibrates inside. The longer lengths of piping produce lower notes, because long columns of air vibrate more slowly. The shorter lengths produce higher notes.

GOOD VIBRATIONS
Hitting piano keys makes wooden hammers strike the piano's steel strings. Each of the strings plays a different note. The long, heavy strings produce low notes, while the shorter, lighter strings make high notes.

White light

Most light sources, including the Sun and torches, give out 'white light'. It is given this name because it seems to have no colour. In fact, white light has more colour than any other type of light. White light is a mixture of many colours, from red to blue. In some situations, all the colours separate out to produce a continuous band of colour called the white light spectrum. For example, a rainbow forms when raindrops separate sunlight into a spectrum.

Compact spectrum

You can produce a spectrum with a compact disc. Take care when handling this not to touch or scratch the shiny surface.

YOU WILL NEED   ▶ 10
◆ A COMPACT DISC
◆ A TORCH
◆ KITCHEN FOIL

1 Make a hole about 0.5cm in diameter in the middle of the foil. Wrap the foil over the front of the torch. Make sure that the hole is over the middle of the torch.

2 Place the compact disc on a table, with the writing facing downwards.

3 Turn on the torch and hold it so that light reflects off the compact disc and into your eyes. You will need to have the compact disc between you and the torch, and point the torch diagonally downwards.

What's going on?
The surface of a compact disc is covered with very small dents called pits. These cause each colour of light to reflect at a slightly different angle, producing the spectrum.

Home-made rainbow

Fill the plant sprayer with water, and set the spray to produce a fine mist. Stand with your back to the Sun. Try to face something dark, like a large bush. This experiment works best in the morning or the evening, when the Sun is not very high in the sky. Spray water in front of you. You will see a band of colours from red to violet (the spectrum) – your very own rainbow!

Can you see a rainbow?

YOU WILL NEED
5
◆ A WATER SPRAY FOR SPRAYING PLANTS
◆ A SUNNY DAY

What's going on?

You should be able to see the seven main colour regions in the spectrum – red, orange, yellow, green, blue, indigo and violet.

FLASHBACK

Rainbow man

The first person to understand white light was English scientist Isaac Newton. In 1666, he performed a famous experiment in his room in Woolsthorpe, Lincolnshire. As many people had done before him, he used a glass prism to produce a spectrum of colours. Before Newton, people believed that the colours were added to white sunlight. Newton was the first to realise that all the colours are present in the sunlight, and the prism simply separates them all out.

I CAN SEE A RAINBOW...

You can see the white light spectrum in a rainbow. In very bright sunshine, you can sometimes see a second rainbow above the main one. The colours are reversed in the second rainbow, with violet at the top.

Coloured light

A theatre stage can be lit up with coloured lights, by shining a white spotlight through a coloured filter. The brake lights at the back of a car look red because they shine through a red plastic filter. Filters remove certain colours from white light, but allow the rest of the spectrum through. Some light sources produce only certain colours of the spectrum.

YOU WILL NEED
◆ A GLASS BOWL FILLED WITH WATER
◆ A TORCH
◆ MILK
◆ A TEASPOON

10

Make your own sunset

Have you ever wondered why the Sun appears orange at sunset? As white light from the Sun passes through the air, the blue and green parts of the spectrum are scattered in all directions. Only the red, orange and yellow light gets through.

3 Shine the torch through the water again. What colour is the light now?

1 Shine the torch straight through the bowl of water towards you. What colour is the light?

How does the torch light change when the milk is added?

2 Add about half a teaspoon of milk to the water, and stir thoroughly.

What's going on?

Tiny particles of fat in the milk scatter blue and green light more than they scatter other colours. The same thing happens to the blue and green parts of sunlight as it passes through the air.

See red

Make the room dark. Hold a compact disc underneath and in front of the red 'stand-by' light of the electrical device. What colours do you see?

YOU WILL NEED
◆ AN ELECTRICAL DEVICE THAT HAS A RED 'STAND-BY' LIGHT (EG TV)
◆ A COMPACT DISC

5

What colours are in different light sources?

What's going on?
Some light sources only give out certain colours of the spectrum. Many electrical devices have red 'stand-by' power lights, which produce only red light. This is why you will not see a spectrum.

Lose the blues

Make a spectrum using a compact disc (see page 94). Hold the yellow folder between the torch and the compact disc. This makes the torch light yellow. Is the spectrum the same?

YOU WILL NEED
◆ A CLEAR YELLOW PLASTIC FOLDER
◆ A TORCH
◆ KITCHEN FOIL
◆ A COMPACT DISC

10

What's going on?
When you shine white light through a yellow filter (your plastic folder) orange, red, yellow and green light pass through it. These are the colours of the spectrum that will appear on the compact disc. The torch light appears yellow because the folder absorbs the blue, indigo and violet light.

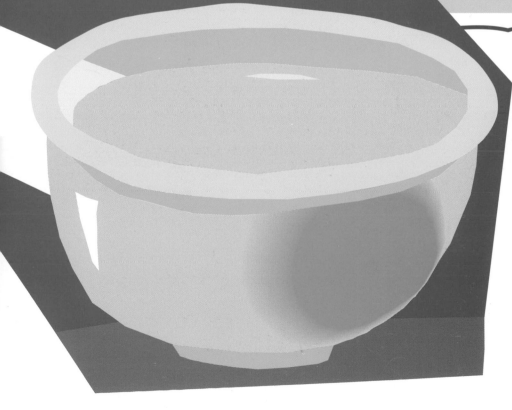

COLOURED TUBES
The coloured writing on advertising signs is created by glass tubes filled with different gases. These tubes often include the gas neon, which gives off orange and red light.

Hearing sound

When sound waves enter your ear, they make a tiny membrane of skin vibrate. These vibrations pass deep into the ear, where they are detected by nerves that send messages to the brain. Sources of sound that are very loud or are close to us make the membrane vibrate more than those that are quiet or far away. If we hear sounds that are too loud, our ears can be permanently damaged.

What's in ear?

When the eardrum moves to and fro, it vibrates three tiny bones (the smallest in your body). The last bone vibrates another membrane, in an organ called the cochlea. The cochlea is filled with fluid and is lined with tiny hairs. The vibrations pass through the fluid, and vibrate the hairs. The hairs are attached to nerves that pass on the information about the vibrations to your brain.

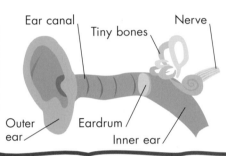

Ear canal   Tiny bones   Nerve

Outer ear   Eardrum   Inner ear

Ear drum

Sound makes a stretched rubber band vibrate, in exactly the way it causes your eardrum to vibrate.

YOU WILL NEED

10
- A BALLOON
- SUGAR (GRANULATED)
- A GLASS OR PLASTIC TUMBLER
- SCISSORS
- AN ELASTIC BAND

1 Cut the balloon and open it out to form a sheet of rubber large enough to fit over the top of the tumbler.

2 Stretch the rubber sheet over the top of the tumbler, and fix it to the tumbler using the elastic band so that the sheet stays taut.

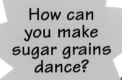
How can you make sugar grains dance?

What's going on?

The sound waves hitting the rubber sheet cause it to vibrate, just as when sound hits your eardrum. You can see this because the sugar grains dance up and down.

3 Sprinkle a few sugar grains onto the rubber sheet. Now shout or make other loud noises, close to the rubber sheet. What happens to the sugar?

Cloth ears

Play some fairly loud music, and hold the yoghurt pots over your ears. The pots absorb some of the sound, and the music does not sound so loud. Squash one sock into each yoghurt pot and hold the pots over your ears once again.

How does the music sound now?

YOU WILL NEED
◆ TWO CLEAN SOCKS
◆ A CASSETTE RECORDER
◆ TWO CLEAN, EMPTY YOGHURT POTS

5

What's going on?

The music sounds quieter because the plastic cups and the socks absorb some of the sound waves, so fewer of them reach your ears. Very loud sounds can damage your ears. People who are regularly exposed to loud noises, like factory workers, wear ear protectors that are specially designed to absorb sound.

LOUD AND QUIET

When a rocket takes off, it makes incredibly loud sounds. If you stood nearby, the sound would hurt your ears. A few kilometres away from the rocket, however, the sound is not so loud. Sound is louder the closer you are to its source, because the sound spreads out as it travels.

Seeing light

Light from light sources, or light that has reflected off other objects, enters our eyes through a lens (see pages 110–111). The lens forms a picture, called an image, at the back of the eye. The back of the eye is connected to the brain by a bundle of nerves. Our eyes hold an image of what we see for about a quarter of a second after the light has entered our eyes.

Model of the eye

To see how the eye forms an image, make a simple model, using a balloon.

YOU WILL NEED
◆ A BALLOON
◆ A SQUARE OF CARD
◆ SCISSORS
◆ A TORCH
◆ A MAGNIFYING GLASS
◆ STICKY TAPE

15

1 Fill the balloon with water from the tap until the balloon is about 10cm in diameter. Tie the balloon, so that the water cannot escape.

2 Cut a piece of card to fit over the front of the torch. Cut an arrow-shaped slit in the card, as shown, and stick the card to the front of the torch.

3 Hold the magnifying glass right in front of the balloon. Now point the torch at the balloon and turn it on.

FLASHBACK

Ideas about seeing
Most people in Ancient Egypt and Ancient Greece thought that when we looked at something, some kind of visual rays came out of our eyes, bounced off objects and then back into our eyes.

What's going on?
You should see an image of the arrow at the back of the balloon. The image is upside down, or inverted, because the magnifying glass makes the light rays cross over each other as they pass through the balloon. Images in the eye are inverted, too, but the brain interprets them so we see them the right way up.

Fooling the eye

In a dark room, turn on the lamp and hold the compact disc underneath the bulb. Look closely at the spectrum this produces. Is it a complete spectrum? What colours are missing?

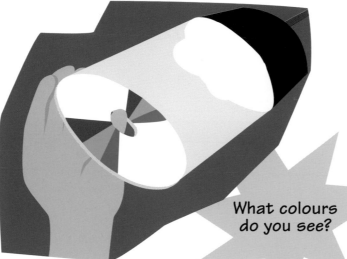

YOU WILL NEED 5
◆ A COMPACT DISC
◆ A LAMP WITH AN 'ENERGY SAVING' BULB

What colours do you see?

What's going on?

Fluorescent lamps, such as 'energy saving' light bulbs, appear white. But they do not produce all the colours of the spectrum, like the Sun or an incandescent lamp does. They fool the eye into seeing white, by producing red, green and blue light.

Only three colours

Turn on the television, and look closely at the screen using a magnifying glass. It has three types of dot – red, green and blue ones.

YOU WILL NEED 5
◆ A TELEVISION
◆ A MAGNIFYING GLASS

What's going on?

Believe it or not, all of the colours you see on a colour television screen are produced by mixing light of just three colours.

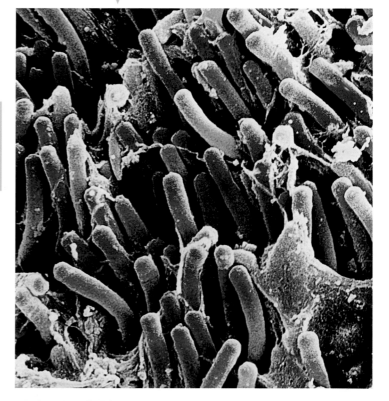

LOOK INTO MY EYES
At the back of your eye are cells that are sensitive to light. These cells send signals along nerves to your brain. Some cells are sensitive to red light, some to green, and some to blue.

101

Reflecting sound

When sound hits a solid object it bounces off, or reflects, just like a ball thrown against a wall. The reflected sound is called an echo. Sound travelling underground – seismic waves – reflects off layers of rock. Recording these underground echoes can tell us much about the nature of those rocks. This is called seismic surveying.

What angle?

Using two kitchen foil tubes, find out how the sound of a ticking watch reflects off a surface.

YOU WILL NEED
◆ A WATCH THAT TICKS
◆ TWO KITCHEN FOIL TUBES
◆ A HARD BACK BOOK

10

1 Open the book slightly, and stand it about 30cm from the edge of a table. Lay one tube on the table, with one end next to the book.

2 Hold the watch near to the other end of the tube. Some of the sound made by the watch will travel down the tube and reflect off the book.

3 Place your ear at one end of the other tube and listen for the reflected sound of the ticking watch. Where do you have to place the tube?

What's going on?
The sound of the watch travels down the tube and reflects off the book. You should be able to hear the ticking sound at only one position.

Bouncing waves

You can experience bouncing sound for yourself! Go outside, close your eyes, and say 'Hello!' quite loudly. Move a book in front of your face, about 20cm away, with the cover facing you, and say 'hello' again. Can you hear the difference? What happens if you use a woollen jumper instead of the book?

Do both of these objects reflect the sound?

What's going on?
The sound waves from your voice are reflected off the book. The jumper does not reflect the sound so well. Air pockets trapped inside the wool soak up most of the sound.

FLASHBACK

Finding their way

About 200 years ago, Italian priest and biologist Lazzaro Spallanzani came up with a very strange idea — that bats find their way around, and even hunt, using echoes. More than 100 years later, Spallanzani's idea was shown to be correct. Bats, dolphins and a few other animals do produce high-pitched sounds, and find their way around by listening to the echoes. This is called echolocation.

CONCERT HALL
Sounds made by musicians in a concert hall bounce off the walls and ceiling, causing repeated echoes, or reverberation. Too much of this can spoil the sound, so absorbent materials like curtains are used to reduce the echoes.

Reflecting light

The Moon does not produce any light of its own, and yet at Full Moon, it is almost light enough to read a book! The light that reaches Earth from the Moon is sunlight that has reflected off the Moon. Light reflects off most things, but much better off white and silvery objects than off dark ones. Some materials reflect only certain colours of light, which is why they appear coloured.

Moon shapes

It is easy to demonstrate why the shape of the illuminated Moon changes from night to night.

1 Tape one end of the string to the ball. Now, make the room dark.

2 Stand in the centre of the room and hold the string so that the ball is just higher than head level and in front of you, suspended in the darkness, like the Moon in space.

What does the tennis ball look like as you turn around?

YOU WILL NEED
◆ A TORCH
◆ A TENNIS BALL
◆ STRING ABOUT 15CM LONG
◆ STICKY TAPE
◆ A FRIEND

15

3 Ask a friend to turn on the torch and shine it at the ball. Now turn around slowly. What do you see?

What's going on?

In this experiment, the ball is a model of the Moon, the torch is the Sun and you are the Earth. The Sun always illuminates half the Moon, and the Moon travels around the Earth once every month. When the Moon is between the Earth and the Sun, we cannot see any reflected light. We call this New Moon. When the Earth is between the Sun and the Moon, we can see the whole face of the Moon. This is Full Moon.

Black and white

Place the two sheets of paper next to each other on a table next to a wall. Make the room dark, and shine the torch on to the white paper. You should see a patch of light on the wall. Now, shine the torch at the black paper.

What's going on?

The white paper reflects much more light on to the wall than the black paper does. Supermarket checkout scanners make use of this fact – a laser reflects off the black and white lines of the barcodes, and a sensor detects the reflected light.

Reflecting colours

Make the room dark, and hold the jumper next to the wall. Shine the torch at the jumper, so that light reflects off the jumper. You should see a patch of coloured light.

What's going on?

White light from the torch is a mixture of many colours. The red jumper only reflects the red light from this mixture.

FLASHBACK

Moon mirror

In 1971, astronomers in America bounced a laser beam off a mirror that astronauts had left on the Moon. By timing how long the light took to return, they worked out the distance to the moon to an accuracy of just a few metres.

ROAD REFLECTOR SIGN

Some road signs are made from materials that reflect light from the headlights of approaching traffic. Different parts of the sign reflect different colours, giving drivers a clear bright image of hazards ahead.

Mirrors

Have you ever caught your reflection in a shop window? Any shiny surface can act as a mirror, but the mirrors in a bathroom or in your bedroom at home reflect all of the light that falls on them. The picture, or image, in a mirror is reversed – right becomes left and left becomes right. Curved mirrors can make things become reversed, too. They can also make things look bigger, smaller or even upside down.

Seeing it both ways

A piece of clear plastic can act as a mirror – on both sides.

1 In a dark room, sit or stand facing your friend, about one metre away from him or her.
Hold the plastic vertically, halfway between you.

YOU WILL NEED
- A FLAT SHEET OF CLEAR PLASTIC FROM A PICTURE FRAME
- A TORCH
- A FRIEND

10

Which of the faces you see is a reflection, and which is not?

2 Turn on the torch and shine it at your face. You should see a reflection of yourself in the plastic. What does your friend see?

3 Ask your friend to shine the torch on his or her face. Now you should see your friend's face, because the light has bounced off it and passed through the plastic. But what does your friend see?

What's going on?

Most of the light that hits a clear plastic or glass surface passes through – this is why you can see your friend in step 3. Some light reflects off the plastic surface, and when there is no light passing through from the other side, you can see the reflected light. This is why you see yourself in step 2.

Magic window picture

Face a window and hold the paper up in front of your face. Now hold the mirror so that it faces away from you and light from the window reflects on to the paper. Make the distance between the mirror and the paper about 15cm. You should be able to see an image of the window on the paper. Alter the distance between the mirror and the paper if you do not see the image straight away.

YOU WILL NEED
◆ A MAGNIFYING MAKE-UP OR SHAVING MIRROR
◆ A PIECE OF WHITE PAPER

10

Can you produce an image on paper with your mirror?

What's going on?

Because the mirror curves inwards, light is brought together, or focussed. This is how it is possible to produce a bright image on the paper.

Reflect on this

Hold the mirror close to your face. The image will be large and the right way up. Scary! Now get your friend to hold the mirror at arm's length, between one and two metres from your face. This time, the image will be smaller and upside down, or inverted.

YOU WILL NEED
◆ A MAGNIFYING MAKE-UP OR SHAVING MIRROR
◆ A FRIEND

5

What's going on?

Mirrors that are used to help people shave or do their make-up are curved inwards (they are called concave mirrors). A concave mirror produces an enlarged view of an object but only if the object is held close to the mirror.

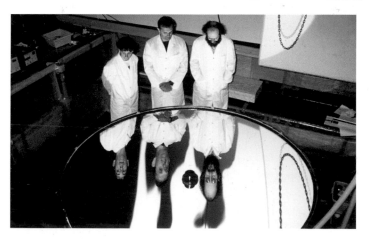

LIQUID MIRRORS
Believe it or not, this mirror is made of liquid metal (mercury). It is going to be used in a telescope. Most telescopes use curved mirrors made of glass or solid metal. This liquid one actually makes a better reflecting surface because mercury produces a perfect dish shape, reflecting all the light that hits it.

Bending light

At the swimming pool, you may have noticed that people swimming underwater look different from how they look out of the water. Light that has reflected off their bodies bends as it leaves the water. This bending of light is called refraction, and happens whenever light passes from one transparent substance to another.

Watch it bend

In this experiment, you can watch a beam of light bending as it enters a bowl of water.

1 Cut a piece of card that will cover the front of the torch. Make a slit in the middle of the card, about 0.5cm wide. Tape the piece of card over the torch.

2 Add a few drops of milk to the water and mix it in well.

YOU WILL NEED
- A TORCH
- CARD, STICKY TAPE AND SCISSORS
- A GLASS BOWL FILLED WITH WATER
- MILK

15

Why does the beam of light bend as it enters the bowl?

3 Make the room dark and shine the torch into the bowl at an angle. Vary the angle, and watch the path of light inside the milky water.

What's going on?
The milk in the water allows you to see the path of the light. You will see the light bend as it enters the bowl. This is because as the beam of light moves from air into the glass and milky water, it changes direction slightly.

Now you don't see it...

Using the modelling clay, attach the coin to the bottom of the saucepan at the opposite side from you. Move your head to the height where the coin just disappears from view. Slowly fill the pan with water. The coin slowly comes into view, without you having to move your head!

YOU WILL NEED
- A SAUCEPAN
- MODELLING CLAY
- WATER
- A COIN

5

Why does it look as if the coin moves under the water?

What's going on?
Refraction occurs when light passes from water to air. This can change the way things look under water.

More or less

Find somewhere lit up by bright sunlight. If it is not sunny, use the torch. Fill the dish with water, and place it where light shines into the water. Stand the mirror against one end of the dish, sloping as shown. Now hold the paper vertically in front of the dish, so that light reflecting off the mirror hits it. You may even see a patch of light on the wall.

YOU WILL NEED
- A SUNNY DAY OR A TORCH
- A FLAT MIRROR
- A FLAT DISH
- WATER
- WHITE PAPER

10

What's going on?
Sunlight (or light from the torch) is a mixture of many colours. Each colour of light refracts at a slightly different angle, so the colours spread out, forming a bright spectrum of colours which you see reflected on the paper.

AFTER IMAGE
Believe it or not, this photograph was taken after the Sun had set! It was possible because light refracts as it passes from the vacuum of space into the atmosphere. Light from the Sun hits the top of the atmosphere, and refracts downwards towards people on the ground.

Lenses

You may know that cameras, binoculars, slide projectors and microscopes use lenses. Have you ever wondered how a lens works? Lenses are specially shaped pieces of transparent material (usually glass) that can make things look bigger, smaller, nearer or farther away than they really are, or even upside down. And all because light refracts as it passes through the lens.

Slide projector

A lens can project an image on to a wall. You can even use a lens to make a simple slide projector, making a shape appear much bigger than its real size.

FLASHBACK

Eyeglass

Some people wear contact lenses to correct their vision. Contact lenses were invented in 1887 by a German inventor, Adolf Fick. They were made of glass and were very uncomfortable. Modern plastic lenses were introduced in 1948, and today, even disposable contact lenses are available.

YOU WILL NEED ▶ 10
- A MAGNIFYING GLASS
- A DESK LAMP
- A PIECE OF PAPER WITH A SHAPE CUT FROM IT

1 Make the room dark. Turn on the lamp and hold the paper over it. Do not hold it too close, as the lamp could be hot.

What's going on?

Light from the lamp passes through the paper and then it refracts as it passes through the magnifying glass. An image of the shape will only form on the wall or ceiling if the magnifying glass is at just the right distance from the paper.

Can you see a shape on the wall or the ceiling?

2 Now, hold the magnifying glass about 10cm above or in front of the paper. You should see an image of the cut-out shape on the ceiling or the wall.

What magnification?

Draw a line 1cm long on the paper. Look at the line through the magnifying glass and try to draw how big the line looks. Measure the line you have drawn.

1cm

What's going on?
A magnifying glass is a type of lens used to look at very small things. The length of the line (in cm) is the magnification of the magnifying glass. If the line was 2.5cm long, your magnifying glass has a magnification of 2.5x.

Water lens
Place the water on a picture in the magazine. Look at the picture through the drop. What do you see?

What's going on?
A drop of water is a simple lens. It can make things look bigger (magnify them) or make them look as though they are far away. Light from an object passes through the water and refracts, making an image of the object. The type of image depends upon whether the object is far from or close to the lens.

A FARAWAY LIGHT
The glass around the light in a lighthouse is made up of a series of glass rings shaped like a lens. This concentrates the light, forming a powerful beam that can be seen over long distances.

Recording sound and light

It is easy to take for granted photographs, television, film, and sound recordings of people talking or our favourite music. When sound hits a microphone, the microphone produces an electric current that flows back and forth in the same way as the vibrations of the sound. Light is normally recorded on a light-sensitive film in a camera. Camcorders and digital cameras contain an electronic device called a charge coupled device, or CCD. Like a microphone, it produces an electric current.

Make a microphone

If you have a cassette player that has a microphone socket, you can use a home-made microphone to record the sound of your own voice! Ask an adult to help you collect the things you need, and to help you put the experiment together.

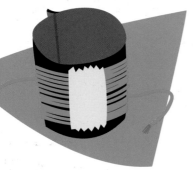

1 Wrap the wire around the canister at least 30 times, leaving about 10cm free at each end.

2 Tape the wire to the canister to stop it from moving. Twist the ends of the wire around the ends of the cable that is attached to the jack plug.

3 Plug the jack plug into the microphone socket of the cassette player and insert the cassette.

4 Start the machine recording, hold the magnet just inside the open end of the canister, and shout as loudly as you can into the canister.

The TALKIES

When you go to the cinema, you can hear the voices of the actors in the film, and music and sound effects, too. The first films had no sound – they were 'silent movies'. The first 'talking picture', or film with sound on general release was 'The Jazz Singer', released in 1928. Audiences at the time were stunned to hear the voice of the star of the film, singer Al Jolson, whose first words in the film were 'You ain't heard nothing yet'.

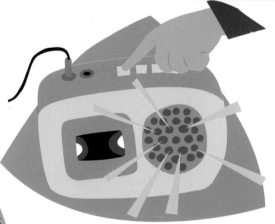

5 Stop and rewind the tape. When you play back at loud volume, you should be able to hear your voice, very faintly, recorded on the tape.

What's going on?

The sound of your voice vibrates the film canister and the coiled wire. Since there is a magnet inside the coil, this causes a small electric current to flow backwards and forwards in the wire. The current is a copy of the vibrations produced by your voice.

Make your own photograph

Cut away some shapes in the piece of black paper. In a darkened room, take a piece of photographic paper, and lay the black paper and your chosen objects on it. Point the lamp at the paper, turn it on, and leave it for a few minutes. Switch the lamp off, and take the objects off the paper. You have your own home-made photograph!

YOU WILL NEED
- A PACKET OF PHOTOGRAPHIC PAPER
- A PIECE OF BLACK PAPER
- A LAMP
- A PENCIL
- SCISSORS
- A SELECTION OF SMALL, FLAT OBJECTS

15

What happens to the picture after a few minutes?

What's going on?
The photographic paper contains chemicals which are sensitive to light. The parts the light reaches change, but the parts covered by the objects and black paper do not.

DIGITAL CAMERA
A recent invention of the electronics industry is the digital camera. Inside a digital camera is a CCD (charge coupled device). Light passes through a lens in the camera, forming an image on the CCD. The image is converted into a pattern of electric currents that can be read by a computer, and displayed on a computer screen.

ELECTRICITY
AND MAGNETS

Sarah Angliss

Getting started

Every time we switch on a light or turn on the TV, we are using electricity. When we close the fridge door or play a tape, we use magnetism. If you've ever wanted to know what electricity and magnetism are, how they work and how we use them, then this section of the book is for you. It is packed with activities and things to make. Before you start, read these pages carefully – they give you lots of useful advice. A few minutes' reading now could save you hours of bother later!

Are you well connected?

If you try the electrical activities on pages 122-149, you'll find electricity only flows between things that are properly stuck together. So when you build a circuit, make sure it has really good connections.

Ask an adult to strip the plastic off the ends of your plastic-coated wires. Electricity can only flow through the bare metal – it does not flow through plastic.

Fix a wire to the terminals of a battery with sticky tape or modelling clay. Make sure the metal part of the wire touches the metal part of the battery.

The right stuff

To try out most of the activities in this section, you only need a few everyday things like batteries, spoons, lemons and paper clips. Sometimes, you'll need more unusual items like iron filings, wire wool and mini-lightbulbs. Try your local toy or hobby shop for these.

Mini-lightbulbs that screw in to a base like this are the easiest sort to use, or you can use bulbs without a base.

For most of the activities, any small battery will do. Put it in a radio to make sure it isn't flat!

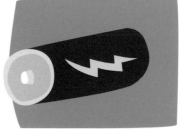

You will also need several lengths of plastic-coated (insulated) wire.

Try to get two straight bar magnets like this.

116

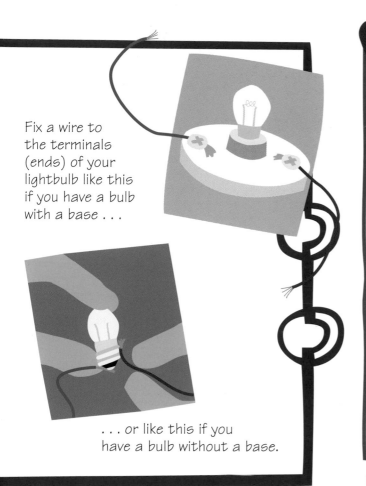

Fix a wire to the terminals (ends) of your lightbulb like this if you have a bulb with a base . . .

. . . or like this if you have a bulb without a base.

Warning

Never experiment with mains electricity (the sort that comes out of plugs and sockets at home or school). It is thousands of times more powerful than a small battery. It can kill.

Never play near overhead pylons or electricity substations. Even when you're not touching them, electricity can jump from them and kill you.

Stuck for words?

If you come across a word you don't understand, or you just want to find out a bit more, have a look in the Glossary on pages 150–157.

Clock symbol

The clock symbol at the start of each experiment shows you approximately how many minutes the activity should take. All the experiments take between 5 and 30 minutes. If you are using glue allow extra time for drying.

10

Having problems?

Don't worry if you have trouble with some of the activities in this book.

If things don't seem to be working, read through each step of the activity again, then have another go.

Remember, even the greatest scientists had problems with their experiments. Take J J Thompson, for example, the scientist who discovered the electron. He was so clumsy, his students would never let him go near his own equipment!

What a tingle!

Electricity, is a form of energy – it makes things happen. For instance, it can heat up a toaster or light up a bulb. We usually think of electricity as something that flows through wires. But there's another form of electricity that doesn't flow at all, called 'static electricity'. You can make this by rubbing certain things together, which gives one or other of them something called 'charge'.

Snake charmer

Use static electricity to move things with no hands! Make sure everything you use in these activities is dry.

YOU WILL NEED
- TISSUE PAPER
- A PLASTIC RULER
- A SCRAP OF NYLON FABRIC
- SCISSORS

10

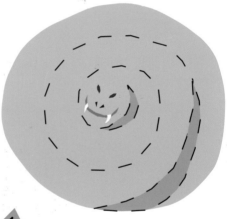

1 Copy this pattern on to the tissue paper and cut it out. Cut along the dotted line, then pull one end to make a spiralling snake. Make more snakes to go with it.

2 Rub a plastic ruler several times with a scrap of nylon.

3 Wave the ruler close to your snakes. Can you lift them up without touching them?

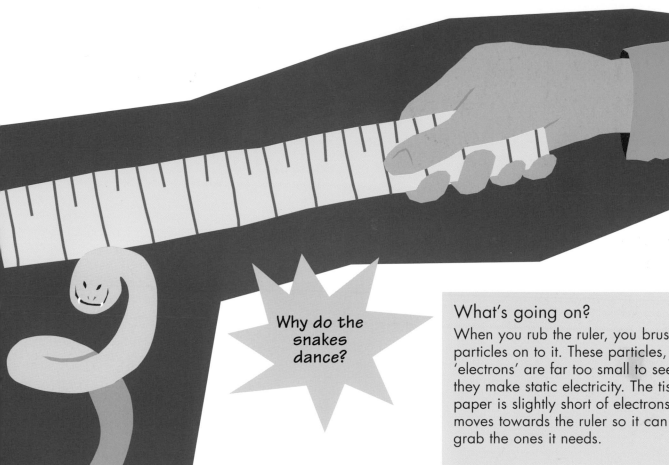

Why do the snakes dance?

What's going on?
When you rub the ruler, you brush tiny particles on to it. These particles, called 'electrons' are far too small to see. But they make static electricity. The tissue paper is slightly short of electrons. It moves towards the ruler so it can grab the ones it needs.

Fashion victim
Listen carefully while you take off some nylon or viscose clothes. If it's dark, look into a mirror while you do this. Do you hear tiny crackles, or see tiny sparks?

YOU WILL NEED
5
- CLOTHES MADE OF NYLON OR VISCOSE
- A MIRROR

What's going on?
The crackles you hear and sparks you see when you take off the clothes are caused by electrons on the move, between your body and your clothes. They are just like mini thunder and lightning!

ELECTRIC STORM
If enough charge builds up in a cloud, it may release itself suddenly in a bolt of lightning. The heat of the lightning makes the air expand, creating a crash of thunder.

Make it move!

An object tends not to keep its charge. If possible, it will dump it on other things nearby. You can make use of this to make things move. Objects attract (pull towards each other) if they have an opposite charge. This lets them get close enough to share electrons so their charge will go away. If they have the same charge, they can't dump electrons on each other and they 'repel' (push each other apart).

What makes the butterfly's wings move?

It's alive!

Charge up a delicate paper butterfly to bring it to life.

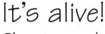

YOU WILL NEED
◆ A METAL PAPER CLIP
◆ AN EMPTY JAM JAR
◆ MODELLING CLAY
◆ KITCHEN FOIL
◆ TISSUE PAPER
◆ A PLASTIC RULER
◆ A SCRAP OF NYLON
◆ SCISSORS

20

1 Uncurl your paper clip. Then bend it into the shape you can see in this picture.

2 Take a scrap of kitchen foil, about the size of the palm of your hand, and roll it into a tight ball. Poke the end of your paper clip into the ball of foil.

3 Rest your paper clip on the rim of the jar, using a piece of modelling clay to keep it in place. Cut a tiny butterfly out of tissue paper. Lay it on your paper clip, inside the jar.

4 Rub a plastic ruler with a scrap of nylon. This will charge it up (see pages 118–119). Watch the butterfly carefully as you bring the ruler very close to the foil ball. Can you see the butterfly's wings move?

What's going on?

The charged ruler has lots of extra electrons which it wants to dump on other objects around it. It can do this when you bring it close to the ball. Electrons find it easy to move through metal so they flow through the ball and paper clip, into the paper. As they give both wings of the butterfly the same charge, the wings repel each other – they open up.

In the bag

Cut a strip from the bag and rub it with the scrap of nylon. This will charge it up by giving it extra electrons. Then rub each of your other objects in turn. Bring them close to the charged plastic strip. If they have lost electrons, they have an opposite charge to the strip so they will be attracted towards it. If they have gained electrons, they will have the same charge as the strip so they will be repelled by it.

YOU WILL NEED
◆ A PLASTIC FOOD BAG
◆ A SCRAP OF NYLON
◆ OBJECTS MADE OF DIFFERENT MATERIALS, EG A METAL FORK, A WOODEN SPOON, A BALL POINT PEN CASING, A CHINA CUP, A GLASS TUMBLER, A PEBBLE AND A PENCIL ERASER

5

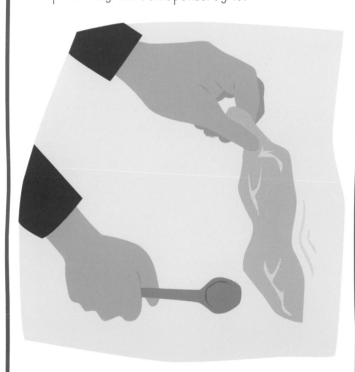

What's going on?

When you rub them, plastic objects, such as the ballpoint pen casing, gain electrons. That's why they repel the strip. Metal objects, such as the fork, lose electrons so they attract the strip. A few objects, including the eraser, do very little to the strip because they hardly pick up any charge at all.

Hair raising

Something has 'charge' when it gains or loses electrons. A thing that has gained electrons will have an opposite charge to something that has lost them. What happens when you charge up your hair by repeatedly passing a plastic comb through it?

YOU WILL NEED
◆ PLASTIC COMB
◆ MIRROR

5

What's going on?

The comb brushes electrons on to your hair. It gives every one of your hairs the same type of charge. As the hairs can't dump their extra charge on each other, they stand on end to keep themselves apart.

AIRSHIP FIRE
In May 1937, the huge *Hindenburg* airship went up in flames when the crew threw some ropes to the ground. They hadn't realised that the weather was stormy and lots of charge had built up on the ship's outer shell. This charge flowed along the ropes, into the ground, causing a spark that set the gas inside the airship alight.

Wire it up

So far, you've only experimented with static electricity – the kind that's made when you brush electrons on to things or rub electrons off them. However, there's another very useful type of electricity that's made by electrons on the move. It's called 'current electricity'. Electrons find it easy to move through metal. Using a battery, you can push them all the way through a metal wire. To do this, you need to make the wire into a complete loop, called a 'circuit', that lets them flow out of the battery then in again.

Bright idea

When current electricity flows through this circuit, it lights up a bulb.

YOU WILL NEED
- A SMALL TORCH BULB (WITH A MAXIMUM VOLTAGE OF 3V OR 4.5V)   **10**
- A 1.5V AA-SIZE BATTERY
- TWO INSULATED WIRES
- STICKY TAPE

1 Ask an adult to strip around 2cm of plastic from each end of your wires.

2 Using sticky tape, fix the bare end of one wire to the silvery knob on the top of your battery. This knob is called the 'positive terminal'.

3 Using some more tape, fix the bare end of your other wire to the silvery base of your battery. This is called the 'negative terminal'.

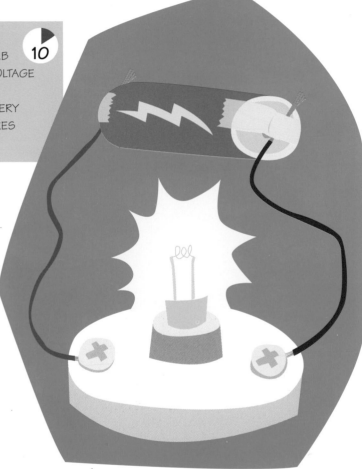

4 Connect your two free ends of wire to the lightbulb. Does your bulb glow?

What's going on?

You have a made a complete circuit. Electrons can flow out of the battery, through one wire, through the bulb, through the other wire then into the battery again. When they flow through the bulb, they make it glow.

Bridge the gap

Follow the steps in 'Bright idea' (left) again to make your torch bulb glow. Ask an adult to cut one of your wires in half to break the circuit. Keep everything else in place. Now ask your adult helper to strip the two free ends of broken wire. Then, using a metal paper clip, touch both free ends of bare wire at the same time. What happens to the bulb?

What happens to the bulb when you break your circuit?

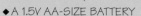
YOU WILL NEED
- A SMALL TORCH BULB (WITH A MAXIMUM VOLTAGE OF 3V OR 4.5V)
- A 1.5V AA-SIZE BATTERY
- TWO INSULATED WIRES
- A METAL PAPER CLIP
- STICKY TAPE

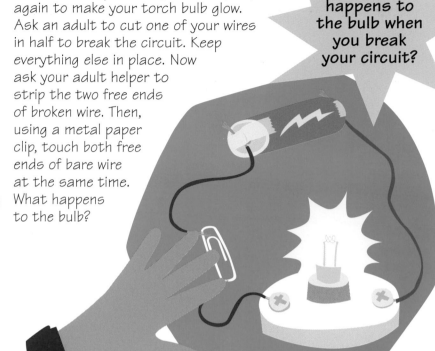

What's going on?

When you break the circuit, electricity can't flow all the way round it so the bulb stops glowing. The metal paper clip can bridge the gap in the broken circuit. When you press it against the two bare ends of broken wire, electricity can flow through it, from one piece of wire to the other. The paper clip completes the circuit, letting the bulb glow. In this way, it works as a switch.

FLASHBACK

Say it with lights

Electricity came into homes at the end of the nineteenth century. At that time, it was an expensive luxury, only seen in the richest city addresses. Electric light was so costly, people only put it in their most important rooms. Some people who could afford only one lightbulb decided to put it in the hall. They left their only electric light on all day — even when they were out — to show it off to passers-by.

PINBALL
The steel ball in this pinball machine bridges the gap between the target and base of the machine. This completes a circuit which makes lights glow and buzzers buzz. The circuit switches on and off in an instant as the ball moves around, making pinball a very fast-moving and exciting game.

Thick and thin

Electricity can flow through any metal wires in a circuit. But it finds it easier to flow through thick wires than thin ones. The amount of electricity flowing through a wire is called the current. If you use a thinner wire, a battery finds it harder to push electricity through it so it will produce a smaller current.

Dim the light

See what happens to your bulb when you put a really thin wire in this circuit.

YOU WILL NEED   **15**
- A SMALL TORCH BULB (WITH A MAXIMUM VOLTAGE OF 3V OR 4.5V)
- 1.5V AA-SIZE BATTERY
- TWO INSULATED WIRES
- A PIECE OF WIRE WOOL
- STICKY TAPE

What happens to the bulb as the wire gets thinner?

1 Follow the steps in 'Bridge the gap' (page 123) to build a circuit that makes a bulb glow when you press down a paper clip.

2 Pull and twist some wire wool to form a strand about 6cm long. Make this strand about the same thickness as your insulated wires.

3 Use your wire wool strand, instead of a paper clip, to bridge the gap in your circuit. Check the bulb glows.

4 Take away about three-quarters of your wire wool to make a strand that's just as long but much thinner. Use it to bridge the gap again. How does your bulb look now?

5 Make your strand even thinner. How does this affect the bulb?

What's going on?
Electricity finds it hard to flow through a circuit that contains a thin strand of wire wool. Your battery can only make a small current in a circuit like this so the bulb glows dimly. When you use an even thinner strand, the battery makes an even smaller current so the bulb glows even more dimly.

Short cut

The wires in this experiment could get warm – so ask an adult to help. Follow the steps in 'Bright idea' (page 122) to build a circuit that makes a bulb glow. Ask an adult to strip the ends of an extra wire. Then touch the bare ends of this wire against the terminals of your battery. Make sure you touch both terminals at once. What happens to the bulb?

YOU WILL NEED
15
- ◆ A SMALL TORCH BULB (WITH A MAXIMUM VOLTAGE OF 3V OR 4.5V)
- ◆ A 1.5V AA-SIZE BATTERY
- ◆ THREE INSULATED WIRES
- ◆ STICKY TAPE

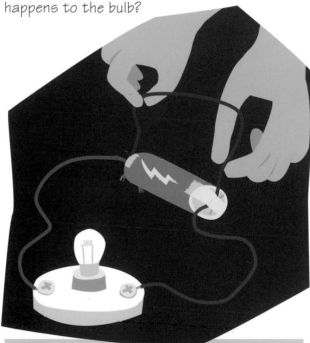

What's going on?

When you put an extra wire across the terminals of your battery, the bulb goes out. Electricity flows through your extra wire, completely by-passing the bulb. If you look closely at your lightbulb, you can see why. Inside the bulb, there's just a thin coil of metal, called a filament, which carries any electricity. Your extra wire is much thicker than this filament, so electricity flows through it far more easily. Your extra wire is a short circuit – an easier route for electric current to take.

Getting warmer

Try 'Dim the light' (far left) again, using only a couple of thin strands of wire wool. Leave the bulb glowing very dimly for at least a minute then feel the wire wool. What do you notice?

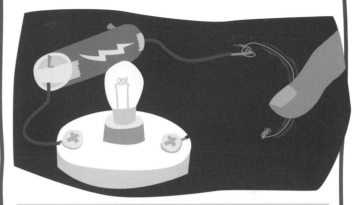

What's going on?

Because electricity finds it very hard to flow through a very thin strand of wire wool, it turns into a different form of energy – heat. This heat makes the wire wool feel slightly warmer to the touch.

WARM GLOW
A lightbulb can turn electricity into light because it contains a very thin filament. The electricity finds it very hard to flow though the filament, so it turns into heat which makes the filament glow white-hot. This is how the bulb makes light.

Go with the flow

Electricity can flow through some substances more easily than others. It can flow very easily through substances called 'conductors', for instance parts made of metal. An 'insulator' is a substance that makes it practically impossible for electricity to flow. Plastics are usually good insulators.

The right stuff?

Here's a handy way to tell apart some everyday conductors and insulators.

1 Follow the steps in 'Bridge the gap' (page 123) to make a circuit with a break in it. Check the bulb glows when you bridge the break with a paper clip.

What's going on?

The bulb glows when you put some objects, such as the metal coin, in the circuit. This is because these objects are conductors. It does not glow when you put other objects, such as the pencil eraser, in the circuit. This is because they are insulators. Conductors, unlike insulators, are made of materials that let electrons flow through them readily. This why they let current flow so easily.

2 Replace the paper clip with another object, for instance a wooden spoon. Does the bulb glow now? Repeat with each of your other objects in turn. Which ones make the bulb glow and which ones don't?

Water and air

You can test two very special substances to see whether they conduct electricity – water and air. To test water, dip your two wires into a small, water-filled saucer. To test air, simply hold your two wires up in the air.

Does water conduct electricity? What about air?

YOU WILL NEED ▶ **10**
- A SMALL TORCH BULB (WITH A MAXIMUM VOLTAGE OF 3V OR 4.5V)
- A 1.5V AA-SIZE BATTERY
- TWO INSULATED WIRES
- STICKY TAPE
- A SAUCER OF WATER

What's going on?

The bulb glows when you bridge the gap in your circuit with water – but not when you bridge it with air. Water, just like metal, lets electricity flow through it. In other words, it's a conductor. Air, on the other hand, is an insulator. Sometimes though, for instance when it is far more powerful, electricity can flow through air. Electricity flows though air to make lightning, for example. You can make enough harmless static electricity to jump a short distance through the air in 'It's alive!' (page 120).

BIRDS ON A WIRE

There is enough current running through this wire to kill. Birds can fly on to the wire and sit on it safely, though, as almost all the current flows through the wire, not the birds. This is because the wire is a much better conductor of electricity than the birds. Never try this yourself. If you reach out to a bare wire, electricity could flow through the wire, through your body and into the ground, and kill you.

127

Power house

A battery is a mini electricity store. When you put it in a circuit, it gradually releases the electrical energy stored inside it. This energy pushes a stream of electrons around the circuit, making an electric current. Believe it or not, you can actually make your own electricity stores, just like batteries, from a few coins and some supplies from the kitchen.

FLASHBACK

Animal electricity

Frogs' legs, not lemons, were used to make the first battery. In a very gory experiment in 1791, the scientist Luigi Galvani noticed the legs of dead frogs twitched when he touched them with two different metals. Another scientist, Alessandro Volta, used this discovery to make a battery from metal discs soaked in salty water.

Fruity tingle

Make enough electricity from a lemon to feel a tingle on your tongue!

YOU WILL NEED
- TWO COINS MADE OF DIFFERENT MATERIALS (TRY A 10p AND 2p)
- A LEMON
- A KITCHEN KNIFE (ASK AN ADULT FOR THIS)

5

1 Ask an adult to cut two small slits in your lemon with a kitchen knife. The slits should be a few centimetres apart and long enough to hold your coins.

2 Now ask your adult helper to strip about 2cm off the ends of your insulated wires. Push a bare end of one wire into each slit. Push a coin into each slit to hold the wires in place. Make sure your coins are made of two different metals.

3 Put the loose end of each wire on your tongue, making sure the wires don't touch. Can you feel anything?

Change the recipe

Lemons aren't the only fruit that will make electricity. Try 'Fruity tingle' (left) again with other types of fruit and vegetables. Change your metal coins too. If you run out of different coins to try, use nails instead. Which home-made battery makes the biggest tingle?

What types of fruit or vegetable make the best batteries?

YOU WILL NEED
◆ COINS AND NAILS MADE OF VARIOUS MATERIALS
◆ DIFFERENT FRUITS AND VEGETABLES
◆ INSULATED WIRES

5

What's going on?

Many combinations of fruit or vegetables and metal will work as mini-batteries. You need to use a food that is acidic (potatoes and pineapples are good) along with two different metals. Some combinations produce a much bigger tingle than others.

4 Pull one wire out of the fruit then repeat step 3 What do you feel now?

What's going on?

Your lemon and coins make a simple battery. They can't produce enough electricity to power a lightbulb, but they should make enough for you to feel a tingle on your tongue. If you pull out one wire, you break the circuit so you don't feel the tingle any more. Inside a real battery, there are two plates made of different metals, just like your coins. These are separated by a type of chemical called an acid, just like the juice of your lemon.

A LIFEJACKET
As soon as this sailor falls into the sea, the salt-water fills a hollow salt-water battery on his lifejacket. This makes the battery work, switching on an emergency light so that the sailor can be seen by rescue teams.

The big push

A battery has to push electricity all the way around a circuit. If a circuit has lots of parts that make it difficult for electricity to flow, the current the battery makes will be very small. This would happen, for instance, if the circuit contained lots of skinny wires. To produce more current in the same circuit, you would need to use a battery that can give electrons a bigger push. The electrical 'push' of a battery is measured in 'volts' (V). A 9V battery, for example, has six times the push of a 1.5V battery.

Does a 9V battery make the bulbs any brighter?

Party lights

See what happens when a battery has to push current through more than one bulb.

YOU WILL NEED
15
- A 1.5 VOLT AA-SIZED BATTERY
- A 9V BATTERY
- UP TO FIVE SMALL TORCH BULBS (EACH WITH A MAXIMUM VOLTAGE OF 3V OR 4.5V)
- UP TO SIX WIRES
- STICKY TAPE

1 Follow the steps in 'Bright idea' (page 122) to make a bulb glow. Check the bulb is glowing and try to remember how bright it looks.

2 Add another bulb to the circuit, like this. Do both bulbs glow? How bright are they?

3 Add more lightbulbs to the circuit. What happens to their brightness? Do they always glow?

4 While you have three or more bulbs in the circuit, swap your battery for a 9V one and see what happens.

What's going on?

As you put more bulbs in this circuit, each one gets dimmer. That's because the bulbs have to share the battery's voltage. The battery has to use some of its voltage to push electricity through each bulb. The current in the circuit reduces every time a bulb is added. If lots of bulbs are added, the current becomes so low, it can't make the bulbs glow at all. A 9V battery pushes more current around the circuit so it can make more bulbs glow.

Dimmer switch

Follow the steps in 'Bridge the gap' (page 123) to make a broken circuit. Bridge the gap in the circuit with a soft propelling pencil lead. Does the bulb glow?

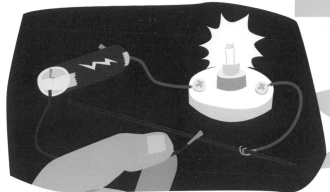

(page 123)

YOU WILL NEED

▶ 10

◆ A 1.5V AA-SIZED BATTERY
◆ A SMALL LIGHTBULB
◆ THREE WIRES
◆ PROPELLING PENCIL 'LEAD'
◆ STICKY TAPE

What happens if you vary the length of the lead between the wires?

What's going on?

As you vary the length of pencil lead between the wires, you change the brightness of the bulb. That's because electricity finds it hard to flow through the lead. The longer the lead is, the more voltage the battery needs to push electricity through it. This leaves less voltage to make the bulb glow.

String them out

Follow steps 1 and 2 of 'Party lights' (far left) to light up two bulbs. Now replace your wires with very long ones. Does this change the brightness of the bulbs?

YOU WILL NEED

▶ 10

◆ A 1.5V AA-SIZED BATTERY
◆ TWO SMALL LIGHTBULBS
◆ THREE SHORT WIRES
◆ THREE VERY LONG WIRES
◆ STICKY TAPE

What's going on?

When you make the wires in your circuit longer, the brightness of the bulbs hardly changes at all. That's because electricity finds it very easy to flow through the wires. No matter how long the wires are, very little of the battery's voltage is used to push electricity through them.

ELECTRIC GUITAR

The volume knob on this electric guitar works just like your dimmer switch. When you turn it, you move two wires nearer and further apart, along a piece of graphite (the material that makes up a pencil lead). This varies the voltage that is available for the amplifier and loudspeaker. When they get more voltage, they make a louder sound.

Neat work

Circuits don't have to be thick and bulky. In fact, you can make a circuit that has wires as thin as a sheet of paper.

A circuit like this can be squeezed into the tightest of spaces – for instance inside a personal stereo or a computer.

Circuit board

Using kitchen foil, you can make a really flat circuit that you can turn into an exciting picture!

FLASHBACK

Mini marvels

Computers changed enormously from the mid 1970s, when the first 'microchips' were sold. No bigger than a postage stamp, each chip contained thousands of wires, etched on to a slither of silicon. Before chips, the computers were made of bulky circuits so they were expensive and huge. A machine with no more computing power than a modern hand-held computer toy took up as much space as several wardrobes!

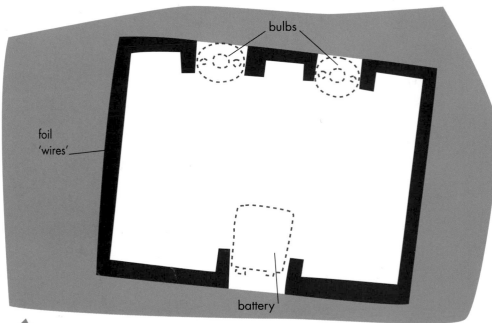

bulbs

foil 'wires'

battery

1 Cut out some neat strips of baking foil, about 2cm wide and 15cm long.

What conducts the electricity in your circuit board?

2 Draw this pattern on to the piece of cardboard. This is the design for your circuit.

3 Stick strips of foil over the parts of the design that are wires.

Glowing masterpiece

Make some holes in the sheet of paper so that when you place it on your circuit the lightbulbs will poke through. Design a colourful picture that will make use of your bulbs, then stick it on to your circuit. Keep the bulbs in place with some re-usable adhesive. When you've finished, stand back and admire your glowing masterpiece!

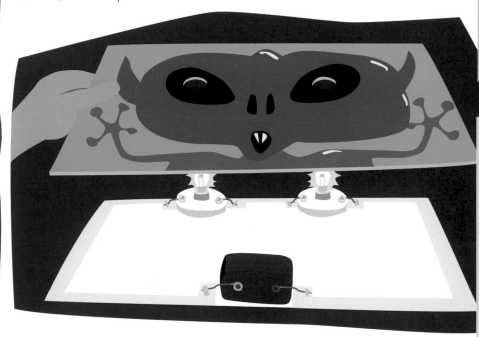

YOU WILL NEED
20
- ◆ THE CIRCUIT YOU MADE IN 'CIRCUIT BOARD'
- ◆ RE-USABLE ADHESIVE
- ◆ A THICK SHEET OF PLAIN PAPER ABOUT 15CM BY 20CM
- ◆ TWO LONG WIRES
- ◆ A CRAFT KNIFE (ASK AN ADULT)
- ◆ CRAYONS, PAINTS OR FELT-TIP PENS

What's going on?

Your circuit is so flat, you have been able to stick it on to the back of a picture. If you like, make a paper clip switch between the battery and circuit board so you can turn your picture on and off as you please (see page 123 for some clues on how to do this).

4 Using short lengths of real wire and some sticky tape, connect your two bulbs and battery to the foil strips. Check your lightbulbs glow.

What's going on?

You have made a very flat circuit by replacing ordinary wires with strips of baking foil. The baking foil conducts electricity just like an ordinary wire. The cardboard backing makes the circuit more robust and helps to keep everything in place.

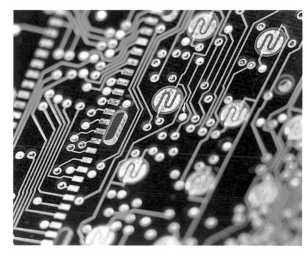

LOOK! NO WIRES

This 'printed circuit board' comes from the inside of a TV remote control. Gadgets like this have very few ordinary wires as most of their circuits look like this. The wires of the circuit, stuck on to the backing, aren't much thicker than a layer of paint.

Branching out

A circuit doesn't have to be made in just one loop. Sometimes, it's handy to give it two or more separate branches. When parts of a circuit are connected in the same loop, they are 'in series'. When they are in two separate loops, connected side by side, they are 'in parallel'. When bulbs are wired in parallel, it's easy to switch them on and off independently of one another.

Ladder of lights

See what happens when you link bulbs together like the rungs of a ladder, in parallel.

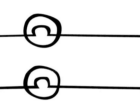

YOU WILL NEED
- A 1.5V AA-SIZED BATTERY
- TWO SMALL TORCH BULBS (WITH A MAXIMUM VOLTAGE OF 3V OR 4.5V)
- TWO SHORT WIRES
- TWO LONG WIRES
- STICKY TAPE
- SCISSORS

15

1 Follow the steps in 'Bright idea' (page 122) to light up a bulb. Use quite short wires to connect the bulb to the battery. Check that the bulb is glowing.

2 Using two slightly longer wires, connect another lightbulb across the terminals of the battery. Do both lightbulbs glow?

3 Ask an adult to cut one of the wires in your circuit. What does this do to one bulb?

What's going on?

This circuit makes both the bulbs glow. That's because each bulb is in its own complete loop. The two bulbs are wired in parallel. Electricity can flow through both loops at the same time. It goes out of the battery, through the bulbs, then back into the battery again. When you cut a wire connecting one bulb to the battery, you turn that bulb off. However, you haven't broken the other bulb's loop, so that one continues glowing.

Upstairs, downstairs

Follow steps 1 to 3 of 'Ladder of lights' (left) to make a circuit that lights two bulbs in parallel. Now break a wire connecting each bulb to the battery. Bridge the gap in each loop of your circuit with a paper clip. Page 123 shows you how to do this.

Page 123 shows you how to do this.

YOU WILL NEED

15

- A 1.5V AA-SIZED BATTERY
- TWO SMALL TORCH BULBS (WITH A MAXIMUM VOLTAGE OF 3V OR 4.5V
- TWO SHORT WIRES
- TWO LONG WIRES
- TWO PAPER CLIPS
- STICKY TAPE

Can you use the paper clips to turn your lights on and off?

What's going on?

You can switch on either bulb, without affecting the other one, simply by pressing down the paper clip switch that's wired to that bulb. That's because the bulbs are wired in parallel. Each of the paper clip switches is wired in series with one of the bulbs.

FLASHBACK

First fairies

The first fairy lights went on sale at the end of the nineteenth century. Unlike fairy lights today, which are strung together in series, these were wired in parallel. This 'failsafe' was important because the early bulbs frequently broke. When one bulb stopped working, the others would carry on glowing.

SKYSCRAPER

Towering over 40 stories high, this skyscraper is illuminated by thousands of lights that are connected in parallel. The lights on each floor make a different branch of a large parallel circuit. When security guards patrol the building at night, they can switch on one branch of the circuit at a time. This makes the lights glow on just one floor, saving electricity.

Feel the force

Magnets vary widely in size, shape and strength, but they can all do two very special things – they can pull objects made of iron or nickel towards them, and they can also attract or repel other magnets. Some magnets occur naturally. They have special magnetic properties as soon as they are mined from the ground. Others are specially made from non-magnets, for instance using electricity. Materials like iron and nickel that are attracted towards a magnet are called 'magnetic materials'.

Jump to it!

Next time someone drops some pins, help them to pick them up with a magnet!

YOU WILL NEED	5
◆A MAGNET	
◆STEEL PINS	

Where do most of the pins stick to the magnet?

1 Bring your magnet close to a small pile of loose pins. Can you pick up the pins with your magnet?

2 Try to pick up a chain of pins with the magnet. How many pins can you pick up this way?

3 Put one pin on the table then gradually move the magnet closer to it. What happens?

What's going on?

Pins stick to the magnet because they are made of steel, a material that contains lots of iron. They are pulled towards it if they are nearby. The magnet pulls most strongly at its ends so that is where most of the pins will stick. Scientists call the ends of the magnet its 'poles'. When a pin sticks to the magnet, it becomes part of the magnet so it can pick up more pins itself. That's why you can pick up a chain of pins.

Is it magnetic?

You can find out which materials are magnetic by trying to pick up a few different objects around your home. (Warning: magnets damage floppy discs, tapes, TVs and computers, so keep them away from these!)

What's going on?

Only objects that contain iron or nickel are attracted to the magnet. You may have found these materials in some of the coins or keys that you tested. The magnet has no effect on objects such as the wooden spoon and pencil eraser because these don't contain any iron or nickel. For the same reason it has no effect on the baking foil – it's made of aluminium.

Can sorter

You can use your magnet to sort steel and aluminium cans for recycling. Using the string and sticky tape, dangle your magnet from the bottom of a chair. Make sure the magnet is about 10cm above the ground. Roll your cans under the magnet, one at a time. Do all the cans roll past the magnet smoothly?

What's going on?

The aluminium cans roll straight past the magnet, but the steel cans slow down. They may even stop moving completely or stick to the magnet. This is because steel is a magnetic material. At refuse centres, cans are often sorted by moving them on a conveyor belt past a line of magnets.

HIGH FLYER
Tilting up and down to steer the plane, this aeroplane wing flap is controlled by a motor that uses a special magnet. Most magnets are mainly made of iron but this one contains lots of boron, a rare metal. This makes it much more powerful than an ordinary magnet. Only a tiny boron magnet is needed to move the wing flap. This keeps the wing as light as possible.

Pole to pole

Every magnet has two distinct poles. To tell them apart, we call them 'north' or 'south' – you can find out more about this on page 146. The area of force around a magnet is called its 'magnetic field'. You can use magnets to create some funny effects!

Opposites attract

The forces between the poles of two magnets can be surprisingly strong – strong enough for you to feel them.

YOU WILL NEED
◆ A RULER
◆ A PENCIL
◆ TWO BAR MAGNETS

5

When do the forces between the magnets feel the strongest?

1 Take a close look at your two bar magnets. There should be paint marks on their ends to tell you which pole is which. They may be labelled 'north' or 'south'. Or they may simply be painted different colours.

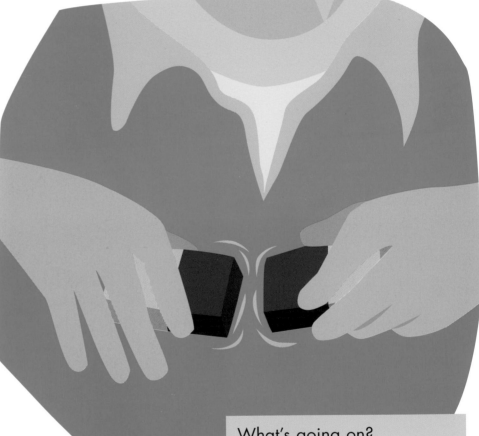

2 Bring two opposite poles of your two magnets close together. Can you feel the force that pulls them together?

3 Turn one of your magnets around so two like poles are facing each other. What force can you feel now? Hold the magnets 3cm apart, then 6cm, then 9cm. How close do the magnets have to be to make a force you can feel?

What's going on?

You feel a strong force between your two magnets when you bring them close together. When different poles are facing, this force attracts the magnets towards each other. When the same poles face each other, this force repels them (pushes them apart). The force gets weaker as the magnets get further apart.

Dancing socks

Put a magnet inside each sock and dangle the socks in the air. Move the socks close together and watch them dance around! Pad the socks out by wrapping each magnet in a couple of layers of paper. Does the trick still work? Now put several layers of paper around the magnets.

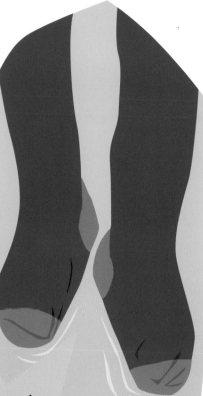

How much paper can you put round the magnets before the trick stops working?

What's going on?

Unless your magnets are very weak, they will be able to attract or repel each other, even though they are covered by your socks. A couple of layers of paper won't weaken the forces between them very much but several layers of paper will. The stronger your magnets, the more paper you can wrap round them before the socks will stop dancing.

Spider stealth

Draw a spider about 5cm across and cut it out. Now tape a paper clip to the bottom of your spider and put it on to the sheet of card. You can make it move wherever you want using a magnet hidden underneath the card!

What's going on?

If your magnet is strong enough, it will pull the paper clip towards it, even though it's separated from it by the card. Anyone watching will see the spider move around in a most mysterious way!

OFF THE RAILS

Magnetic forces between runners on the bottom of the train and the track make this train hover and move forwards. Called a Maglev, the train never touches the rails below it. It travels far more smoothly and quietly than an ordinary train.

Magnetic art

Magnets aren't only useful for making machines and tools. With a little imagination, you can also use them to create magnetic works of art! You can make interesting moving sculptures, like the one below, or fascinating permanent pictures of a magnet's forces.

Freaky pendulum

Three magnets will make this sculpture that swings in the strangest of ways.

YOU WILL NEED
- THREE MAGNETS
- AN IRON NAIL
- STRING
- A CHAIR
- MODELLING CLAY
- STICKY TAPE

10

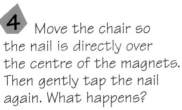
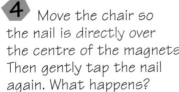

1 Tie some string to the head of your nail. Then dangle the nail from a rung under the chair. Make sure one of your magnets can fit underneath your hanging nail, with a gap of about 1cm.

2 Tap the nail gently and watch it swing to and fro like a pendulum. Make sure there are no magnets near your nail when you do this.

3 Using some modelling clay, fix three magnets to the floor, like this. Make sure the same poles of the magnets are facing each other. The poles should be about 2cm apart.

4 Move the chair so the nail is directly over the centre of the magnets. Then gently tap the nail again. What happens?

What's going on?
When there are no magnets around, the nail swings to and fro smoothly, just like the pendulum of an old-fashioned clock. The only force the nail feels is the force of gravity. When you put the magnets beneath the nail, it swings in a crazy, unpredictable manner. This is because it also feels a force from each of the magnets. As it swings nearer and further from each magnet, the force on it varies continually.

Get the picture

Place your magnet under a sheet of paper. Sprinkle iron filings on the paper. The filings will form a definite pattern because the magnet is under the paper. Put a little paint on your toothbrush then flick the toothbrush with your finger to spray paint on to the paper. When the paint is dry, carefully remove the magnet and filings.

YOU WILL NEED
◆ A BAR MAGNET
◆ IRON FILINGS
◆ PAINT
◆ AN OLD TOOTHBRUSH
◆ A BLANK SHEET OF PAPER

15

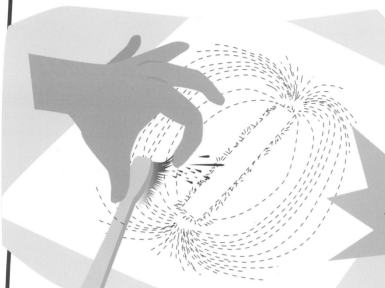

Where do most of the filings settle?

What's going on?

Most filings settle around the poles because this is where the force of the magnet is greatest. Others settle in onion-shaped rings around the magnet. These rings are called 'lines of force'. The pattern of the filings is perfectly symmetrical because the magnet creates exactly the same force at each pole and on each side.

FLASHBACK

Flea circus

Some tricksters in the nineteenth century pretended they had performing fleas. They would entertain people with their flea circuses at theatres and fairgrounds. The tricksters pulled strings and moved tiny metal props around with hidden magnets. This made it look as if the circus contained a team of flea acrobats.

THUNDERBIRD PUPPET

This original Thunderbirds puppet, Scott, has a pair of magnets in his lips. Scott's mouth is normally held closed by a spring, but when his magnets are activated, they create a force which pushes his lips apart so he can 'speak'.

Make your own magnets

Every magnet is made of billions of tiny ones, called 'domains', that are all lined up in the same direction. Other materials have domains too but theirs are all in a jumble. If you have a magnet, you can tease the domains of magnetic materials to make them face the same way. In this way, you can make more magnets of your own.

At a stroke

To turn a paper clip into a magnet, you just have to stroke it the right way.

YOU WILL NEED
◆ TWO STEEL PAPER CLIPS
◆ A MAGNET
◆ MODELLING CLAY

10

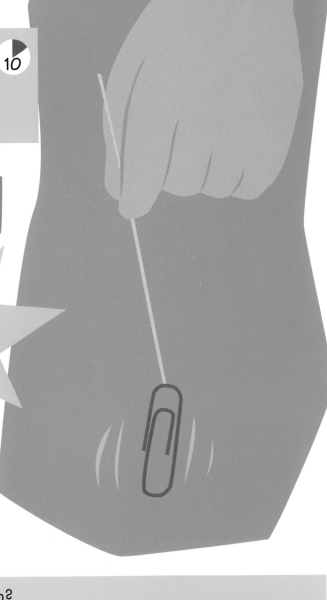

1 Unfurl a steel paper clip and lay it on a firm surface. Fix it in place with some modelling clay.

What makes the paper clip turn into a magnet?

3 Move your magnet out of the way, pick up your steel paper clip and test it. Can you pick up another paper clip with it?

2 Holding your bar magnet in one hand, move it through the air in a loop like this, close to the paper clip. Repeat this several times. Take care to keep your magnet facing the same way. Never change the direction of the loop.

What's going on?

When you stroke your steel paper clip with a magnet, you turn the paper clip into a magnet too. This is because the magnet pulls at the domains of the paper clip until they all face in one direction. The magnet can move the domains around because the domains themselves are microscopic magnets.

Magnetic mobile

YOU WILL NEED
- A MAGNET
- SOME STRING AND A SELECTION OF LIGHTWEIGHT IRON AND STEEL OBJECTS EG STEEL PAPER CLIPS, IRON NAIL AND OLD STEEL KEY.

20

Make a magnetic mobile and see how long it lasts. Follow the steps in 'At a stroke' (left) to magnetise lots of things. Suspend your largest object from a piece of string just above floor level, then link together as many of the other objects as you can. Be careful when using nails in this experiment. Keep the items together using the magnetic forces between them – don't use sticky tape or glue. Check your mobile to see what happens.

What makes magnetism fade over time?

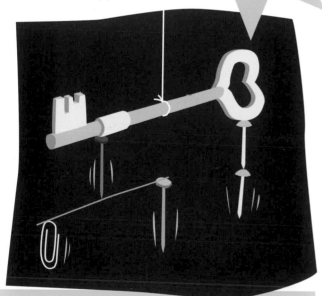

What's going on?
As every part of this mobile is a magnet, you can keep it together without any glue or sticky tape. Over time, the magnetism of your objects will fade. This happens faster if the mobile gets bashed or dropped. Every small shock to the mobile jumbles up its domains a little. This reduces its magnetism. Steel objects stay magnetic far longer than iron objects because their domains are harder to jumble.

Off the menu
Hundreds of years ago, onions and garlic were banned from many ships' rations. Ships navigated using magnetic compasses (see page 146) and crews mistakenly believed that onions and garlic affected magnets! The sailors worried that they would lose their way if the ship's compasses became confused.

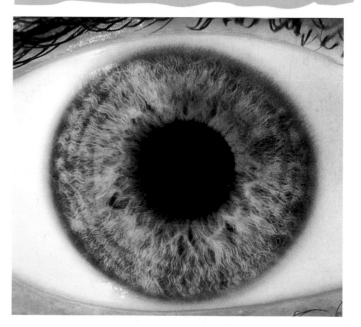

EYE FULL
Magnets can be used to remove some metal objects safely from the eye. The metal can be removed without touching the eye so the eye is far less likely to be damaged. Surgeons usually magnify an eye before they perform the delicate task of pulling any object from it.

Mini-magnets

You can't destroy a magnet just by chopping it in half. That's because the two halves of magnet you are left with will both still have billions of domains that all point in the same direction. These domains will give both halves their magnetism.

Double up

Ask an adult to help you chop a home-made magnet in half – and you'll have two home-made mini-magnets!

YOU WILL NEED
◆ TWO STEEL PAPER CLIPS
◆ A MAGNET
◆ COTTON THREAD
◆ WIRE CLIPPERS OR PLIERS (ASK AN ADULT FOR THESE)

15

1 Follow the instructions in 'At a stroke' (see page 142) to turn a paper clip into a home-made magnet. Check your home-made magnet works.

2 Ask an adult to chop your home-made magnet in half, using wire clippers or pliers.

How does cutting a magnet in half make two magnets?

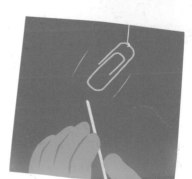

3 Dangle an ordinary metal paper clip from a cotton thread. Hold one half of your broken home-made magnet close to it. Does it attract the paper clip? Repeat this step using the other half of your home-made magnet.

4 Now dangle one half of your broken magnet from another cotton thread. Hold the other half close to it. Can you make the two halves attract each other? What happens if you turn around the half of the magnet that's in your hand?

What's going on?

When you chopped your home-made magnet in half, you made two mini-magnets. That's because each half still has large numbers of domains all facing in the same direction. Each mini-magnet can attract a paper clip. As it has a north and south pole, it can also attract and repel the other mini-magnet. You can cut your home-made magnet into more pieces to make even smaller magnets.

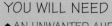

Wipe out

Play an unwanted music tape and stop it about half way through. Take the tape out of the tape player and pull out a loop of tape about 30cm long. Pass a magnet close to the end of the loop of tape. Be careful not to bring it close to the rest of the audio tape. Carefully wind the loop back into the tape then play the tape again. What happens when you reach the part of the tape that was near the magnet?

YOU WILL NEED
◆ AN UNWANTED AUDIO TAPE WITH MUSIC RECORDED ON IT (ASK AN ADULT'S PERMISSION FIRST!)
◆ A TAPE PLAYER
◆ A MAGNET

10

What's going on?

The magnet wiped the sound from part of the tape. Small groups of magnetic granules on the tape store tiny fragments of sound. Each fragment is less than a ten-thousandth of a second long. The granuales have stronger magnetism when a louder sound is stored. When you pass a magnet close to the tape, you overpower the magnetism of each group of granules, wiping out this stored information.

FLASHBACK

Danger music

Playing some of the first magnetic recordings, in the 1930s, was a dangerous business. Rather than using magnetic granules on tape, people stored sound on a piece of magnetised wire. To play back the sound, the wire had to move through a machine at high speed. If the wire snapped, it could break loose, cutting through anything – or anyone – in the area. Listeners had to be ready to make a speedy exit!

COMPUTER HARD DISK
The hard disk in your computer uses magnetism to store words, pictures and other information. Tiny magnets change the pattern of the magnetism to store information as you work, or to wipe it off.

Map it out

Ever since people discovered magnets, they have used them to find their way from place to place. Magnets can be used to navigate because they always turn around to face roughly north. This is because they are affected by the Earth, which itself acts like a very big but weak magnet. A magnet used to find north is called a 'compass'.

Travelling light

This compass, which can fit in a matchbox, is also light enough to float on water.

YOU WILL NEED
- A MAGNET
- A STEEL PIN
- A BOTTLE CORK
- MODELLING CLAY
- A LARGE PLASTIC BOWL
- WATER
- A CRAFT KNIFE (ASK AN ADULT)

15

1 Follow the instructions in 'At a stroke' (page 142) to turn a steel pin into a magnet. Use your magnet to do this.

2 Ask an adult to cut a small disk, about 1cm thick, from the end of your bottle cork using the craft knife. Place the pin on top of the cork. Fix it in place with a tiny amount of modelling clay.

What happens to the pin when you turn the bowl?

3 Fill the bowl with water. Then carefully float the steel pin and cork in it.

FLASHBACK

Stone followers

Magnetite, a type of iron, is a naturally occurring magnet. Tiny fragments of magnetite are often called lodestones, meaning 'leading stones'. They are called this because they can be used to point north, leading the way home. The Chinese were the first to discover that lodestones could be used to navigate. They used lodestones to make the first compasses around 2,300 years ago.

About turn

You can confuse your compass with a magnet. Follow the steps in 'Travelling light' (left) to make a mini, floating compass. Check it points in a north–south direction when it settles. Then bring a magnet a few centimetres away from your compass. What happens?

How can a magnet confuse a compass?

YOU WILL NEED
◆ A MAGNET
◆ ITEMS USED IN 'TRAVELLING LIGHT' (OPPOSITE)

20

What's going on?

As soon as you bring a magnet close to your compass, the compass' poles spin towards the magnet's poles, so the compass stops pointing north. That's because your magnet is much stronger than the Earth's magnetism. The magnet overpowers the Earth's magnetism, confusing the compass.

4 Wait for the steel pin and cork to stop turning. Draw a picture of the pin on a piece of paper. Lie it on the floor and note which way the needle faces.

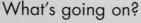

What's going on?

When it stops turning, the magnetised steel pin always lies in the same direction, even if you turn the bowl. That direction is roughly north–south. It does this because its north and south poles are being attracted by the Earth, which itself is a giant, weak magnet. One pole of the Earth's magnetism is roughly north on the map. The other is roughly south.

PIGEON POST
With an amazing sense of direction, pigeons like this can find their way home even after they are moved hundreds of kilometres away. Scientists think homing pigeons are good navigators partly because they can sense the Earth's magnetism.

Pick-up power

Electricity and magnetism are very closely linked. When electricity flows through a wire, it turns the wire into a magnet. Coiled wire concentrates this magnetism so that it is strong enough to pick things up. When you move a magnet near a wire, you make a tiny current. Our homes are full of machines that make use of this connection between electricity and magnetism. We call the link between electricity and magnetism 'electromagnetism'.

Electric magnet

Send electricity through a coil of wire to make a strong magnet. The wires in this experiment could get warm – ask an adult for help.

YOU WILL NEED
- AN IRON NAIL
- A VERY LONG WIRE WITH PLASTIC COATING
- A PAPER CLIP
- A 9V BATTERY
- STICKY TAPE
- STEEL PINS

15

1 Wind the wire tightly around the iron nail at least ten times, holding it in place with sticky tape.

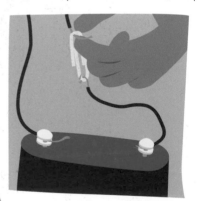

2 Connect one end of the wire around your nail to a terminal of your 9V battery. Connect the other end to the other terminal, and add a paper clip switch (see page 123).

How can an iron nail be turned into a magnet?

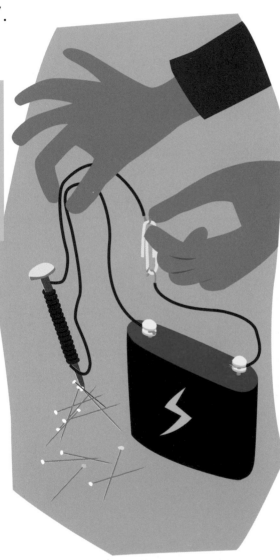

3 Hold the nail over a pile of steel pins. What happens? Remove the paper clip switch to turn the circuit off. What happens now?

What's going on?

When the switch is in place, the iron nail picks up pins. That's because electricity flows through the circuit, turning its wires into weak magnets. As part of the wire is coiled, it concentrates this magnetism. It makes a strong enough magnetic force to turn the nail into a magnet. A magnet like this, that only works when electricity flows around it, is called an 'electromagnet'.

Electric eels

Follow the steps in 'Electric magnet' (left) to make an electromagnet. Then use it to challenge a friend to a game of electric eels. Cut out some eels from tissue paper then stick a tiny piece of wire wool to their heads. Take turns to pick up eels, against the clock, using nothing but your electromagnet. You'll need to use all your skill to turn your electromagnet on and off at the right time. If you pick up one eel, you can keep it. If you pick up two or more, you have to throw them back!

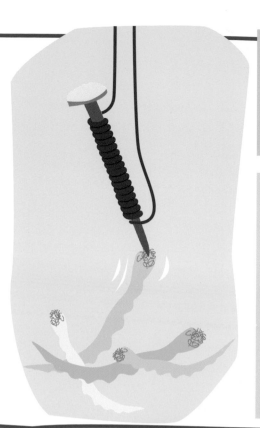

What's going on?
As all the eels have wire wool on their heads, you're able to pick them up with your electromagnet. The nail is only magnetised when the paper clip switch is on. When the clip is switched off, there is no electric current running through the circuit, so there is no magnetism.

FLASHBACK

Moving idea
When the scientist, Michael Faraday, demonstrated the first motor in 1821, he had some trouble convincing people 'electromagnetism' would be so useful. Nowadays, the link between electricity and magnetism enables us to build all sorts of machines that use electricity to control how things move. An electric motor and loudspeaker are just a couple of examples.

AT THE SCRAP YARD
Dumps and scrap yards often have huge cranes that carry electromagnets, just like this. These are strong enough to pick up huge lumps of metal – even whole cars.

Glossary

Acceleration   When an object changes its speed or direction, it is accelerating. Acceleration is measured in metres per second squared (m/s^2).

Air pressure   The pressure caused by the weight of the atmosphere, also called atmospheric pressure. Although it is invisible, air has mass, so it is pulled down by the Earth's gravity. The pressure of the air at the Earth's surface is about ten newtons per square centimetre ($10N/cm^2$). Weather maps show areas of higher or lower air pressure, as these have a strong effect on the weather.

Air resistance   The resistance of air to the motion of objects travelling through it. This resistance happens because moving objects rub against the molecules of the gases that make up the air.

Attract   Two things attract each other if they want to pull themselves closer together. This happens when they have opposite electrical charges (when one has too many electrons and the other has too few). A magnet will attract objects that contain lots of iron. Two magnets will attract each other if the north pole of one is near the south pole of the other.

Balanced forces   Forces that do not cause any change in the motion of an object when they interact are said to be balanced. When you sit on a chair, for example, the force of gravity pulling you down is balanced by the equal and opposite reaction force of the chair pushing you up.

Barcode   Series of numbers with vertical black and white lines often found on the packaging or labels of products. When a barcode is scanned at the checkout, a laser reflects off the lines of the barcode and a sensor detects the pattern of the reflected light. This pattern gives information about that particular product and its price.

Boil   When bubbles quickly grow in a liquid, rise to the surface and burst, releasing vapour. Boiling is the most rapid form of evaporation.

Brittle   Describing solids that snap easily when bent or shatter into pieces when struck. The opposite of tough.

CCD   Short for 'charge coupled device'. A device found in digital cameras that converts an image from the camera lens into a pattern of electrical currents that can be read by a computer and displayed on a computer screen.

Cell   The smallest basic unit in the structure of living things. All cells have a watery jelly-like substance inside them called cytoplasm, and are surrounded by a membrane. Different parts of our bodies are made up of different types of cell. All cells use energy so they can function and reproduce.

Centre of gravity (or centre of mass)   The point in an object where the force of gravity appears to act. If it is suspended from any point on the vertical line passing through its centre of gravity, the object will stay balanced.

Centripetal force The force that causes something to move in a circular path. When you twirl a stone around on a string, you have to pull on the string to keep the stone from flying off in a straight line. The force of the string tugging on the stone is the centripetal force.

Charge Something has charge if it has too many or too few electrons. This could happen because you've rubbed it with another object to make static electricity. Two objects have the same type of charge if they've both lost electrons or if they've both gained them. They have 'opposite' charges if one has gained electrons but the other has lost them.

Chemical A single, pure substance. Salt is a chemical that chemists call sodium chloride.

Chemist A scientist who studies how permanent changes can make new substances. Remember that the people in charge of chemist's shops are called pharmacists. They prescribe medicines.

Cochlea A spiral-shaped part of the inner ear, which contains fluid and thousands of hairs. The fluid and hairs vibrate when sound travels through them, then nerves pick up this information and pass it on to the brain. The brain interprets the signals as sound.

Combustion Another word for burning.

Compass A device that can be used to find out roughly where north is. The most important part of a compass is the pointer, which is a magnet. Like all magnets, the pointer will end up lying in a roughly north–south direction when it's left to swing freely.

Compress To squeeze something so that its volume decreases and it takes up less room than it had before. It is fairly easy to compress gases. It is almost impossible to compress liquids or solids.

Concave mirror A mirror whose reflective surface curves inwards.

Condense To change a gas into a liquid, usually by cooling it.

Conductor A substance that electricity can flow through easily. Metal and water are both good conductors. These are the raw materials of many electrical devices, for instance wires, switches and lightbulbs. Metals such as copper and aluminium are good conductors (see **Insulator**). You may also come across the word 'conductor' when people are talking about things other than electricity. For instance, engineers often ask if a material is a good conductor of heat.

Contract When an object becomes smaller. Most solids and all liquids and gases contract when they cool and their temperatures decrease.

Current A measure of how much electricity is flowing. Current is measured in amps (A). A circuit will have a bigger current if a battery finds it easier to push electricity around it. A larger current means more electrons are flowing through the circuit.

Density How much mass something has in relation to its volume. Density is worked out by dividing a substance's mass by its volume, measured in grams per centimetre cubed (g/cm^3).

Dissolve When a substance disappears as it mixes into a liquid. Salt dissolves in water to make salt solution.

Domains The millions of mini-magnets, far too tiny to see, that make up every material. The domains of a magnet all face in the same direction. Their magnetism will fade if their domains get jumbled, for instance because they have been bashed with a hammer.

Drag An aerodynamic force that resists the forward motion of an object. The shape of the object affects the amount of drag.

Ear defenders Protective coverings for the ears that people wear in noisy places like factories to prevent damage to their hearing. Ear defenders are made of material containing lots of air holes, which help to absorb loud noises.

Eardrum A tiny membrane of skin inside the ear that vibrates when sound waves enter the ear. The vibrations are passed deeper into the ear and are detected by nerves which send messages to the brain, where they are interpreted as sound.

Echolocation A way of finding the position of something by sending out sounds which are reflected back from it. Bats, dolphins and some birds make use of this. They make high-pitched sounds and use the echoes to find their way around.

Elastic A solid that changes shape when squeezed or stretched; it then returns to its original shape when the squeezing or stretching stops.

Electricity The form of energy that makes toasters, house lights, televisions, vacuum cleaners and all other electrical things work. Electricity is created by particles, called electrons, which are far too tiny to see. Electrons make 'current electricity' when they flow through things such as wires and light bulbs. When they are not moving, electrons produce 'static electricity'.

Electromagnet A magnet that only works when electricity flows through it. Most electromagnets are made of a coil of wire, wrapped around some metal to boost its magnetic strength.

Electron A tiny particle that is far too tiny to see. There are one or more electrons in every atom. When electrons flow through things, for instance a wire, they make current electricity. When they rub off one thing and on to another, they make static electricity.

Energy The ability to do work. Work is done whenever a force moves through a distance, so you can think of energy as a 'promise' to do work. There are several kinds of energy, like light, heat, electrical energy and potential energy. Fuels contain energy that is released as heat when they burn. Both work and energy are measured in joules (J).

Evaporate When a liquid changes into a vapour (gas), usually by heating it.

Expand When an object becomes larger. Solids, liquids or gases expand when they are heated and their temperatures increase.

Filament The thin, coiled wire inside a light bulb that makes the bulb glow. Electricity finds it hard to flow through this wire so it turns into another form of energy, heat. This makes the filament glow white hot, producing light through incandescence.

Filter   A clear screen, through which light can pass, that removes certain colours from white light, allowing the rest of the spectrum through.

Filtrate   The liquid part of a suspension that passes through a filter.

Fluorescent   Light given out by some materials when they absorb various kinds of energy. The inside of a fluorescent lamp is coated with a material that absorbs ultraviolet light and changes it into visible light.

Focus   A way of bringing something together and concentrating it in one place, as when light is focussed in a concave mirror.

Force   A push or a pull. Force can do work and make things speed up, slow down or change shape. Forces can also cancel when they push or pull against each other.

Force magnifier   A machanism where a small force moving a long distance causes a big force to move a small distance, for example a door handle.

Forces   The pushes or pulls that can change something's speed, shape or direction. Forces are measured in newtons (N).

Freeze   When a liquid changes into a solid, usually by cooling it.

Frequency   How often something happens. For example, a source of sound that vibrates many times each second has a high frequency.

Friction   The force that resists movement when things slide against each other.

Gears   Toothed wheels used in machines to make one wheel turn another.

Gravitational pull   The pull of one object on another due to the force of gravity. For example, the Earth's gravity keeps satellites such as the Moon in orbit.

Gravity   A force of attraction that pulls everything towards everything else. The strength of attraction depends on the mass of the objects and how far apart they are.

Heat   A form of energy. When heat flows into an object, its temperature increases. The temperature decreases when heat flows out of an object.

Image   A picture or likeness of a person or thing produced from a mirror, through a camera lens or by electrical means on a screen.

Incandescence   Light given out from objects, such as the Sun, because they are hot. An incandescent lamp produces light because its electrical filament becomes hot.

Inertia   The tendency of any object to stay still or move steadily in a straight line unless a force makes it do otherwise. The more mass something has, the greater its inertia.

Insoluble   A substance that does not dissolve in a liquid.

Insulator   A substance that makes it very hard for electricity to flow through it. Wood, paper, glass and plastic are all good insulators. Electric machines and parts are often covered in insulators to make them safe – for instance, wires are often covered in plastic and a television is built inside a plastic box. People also use the word 'insulator' when they're not talking about electricity. For instance, they might look for a material that's a good insulator of heat.

Kilogram   The standard unit of mass. A volume of one litre of water has a mass of one kilogram.

Length   A measurement of the distance between two places. The unit of length is the metre (m). One metre equals 100 centimetres (cm) or 1000 millimetres (mm). One kilometre (km) is equal to 1000m.

Lens   Specially-shaped pieces of transparent material that can make things look bigger, smaller, nearer or farther away. They do this by bending the light as it passes into them and out again.

Lever   A rigid bar that can turn on a pivot or hinge to transmit a force from one place to another. Wheelbarrows, scissors, and the muscles and joints of your body are all examples of lever systems.

Lift   An aerodynamic force caused by the motion of a wing through the air. Lift allows an aeroplane to climb into the air and holds it up during flight.

Lubricant   A substance that reduces the friction between two surfaces.

Luminescence   Light given out from objects, such as fireflies and television screens, produced by means other than heat.

Machine   A device that does work.

Magnet   An object that can pull iron or nickel objects towards it. Magnets can also attract or repel other magnets. Some rocks, like magnetite, are naturally occurring magnets. Other magnets can be made in the laboratory, for instance by stroking iron or nickel with other magnets.

Magnetic field   The area around a magnet where it can attract or repel things. Stronger magnets have a larger magnetic field.

Magnetic materials   Materials that are attracted towards magnets. Iron and nickel are magnetic materials. So are many materials that contain either of these two metals. Steel, for instance, contains lots of iron so it is a magnetic material.

Mass   The amount of matter in an object. The unit of mass is the kilogram (kg). One kilogram is equal to 1000 grams (g). One thousand kilograms is equal to one tonne.

Material   Different kinds of solids. Steel, paper, skin, stone and plastic are all materials. Objects are made by fitting different materials together.

Matter   Anything that has mass and takes up space.

Melt   When a solid changes into a liquid, usually by heating it.

Membrane   A thin, flexible piece of skin which joins or covers parts of a living thing, or separates one part of a living thing from another.

Motion   Motion occurs when something changes its position.

Movement magnifier   A mechanism where a large force moving a short distance causes a small force to move a long distance, for example the pedal that opens the lid of a pedal bin.

Neon   A colourless gas that glows orange and red when electricity is passed through it. It is used in tube lighting for advertising signs.

Nerve   A pathway that carries messages between the brain and other parts of the body.

Newton   Unit for measuring forces. The pull of Earth's gravity on a mass of 1kg is almost exactly 10N.

Parallel   The word used to describe electrical parts that have been wired into two or more separate loops. Each loop lets electricity flow out of the battery, through itself, then back into the battery again.

Permanent   Describing a change that cannot easily be reversed.

Pitch   The way something sounds high or low, like the different notes in a musical scale.

Poles   The two areas of a magnet, usually at its ends, in which the magnet's pull is strongest. If you let a magnet swing freely, one pole will always end up pointing approximately south. This pole is the magnet's 'south pole'. The other, called the magnet's 'north pole', will always end up pointing roughly north. The poles end up pointing in these directions because they are attracted to the north and south poles of the Earth, which is itself a giant magnet.

Potential energy   Energy that is stored. When you lift something up or stretch a spring, you give it potential energy.

Pressure   A measurement of the amount of force pressing on the surface of an object. Your feet and body weight exert pressure on the floor. The pressure of the air inside a balloon keeps the skin stretched outwards. Pressure is calculated by dividing the size of the force by the area it is acting on. It is measured in pascals (Pa) or newtons per square metre (N/m^2).

Prism   A transparent, many-sided block of glass or plastic that can separate light passing through it into the colours of the spectrum.

Pulley   A wheel with a grooved rim. Several can be used together to make it easier to lift a heavy load. This is an example of a force magnifier.

Raw materials   Natural substances that are used to make useful products. Raw materials are extracted from the ground (for example, iron ore and crude oil), from seawater (for example, bromine and iodine for use in medicines) and from the air (for example, oxygen and nitrogen).

Reflection   The bouncing back of light or sound from a surface, for example light from a mirror, or sound from the walls of the inside of a tunnel.

Refraction   The way light bends as it passes from one different substance to another, for example from air to water or from air to glass.

Repel   Two things repel each other if they want to push themselves further apart. This happens when they have the same type of electrical charge (when both objects have too few electrons or both have too many). Two magnets will repel each other if the north pole of one is close to the north pole of another. They will also repel if their south poles are close together.

Saturated solution   A solution that cannot dissolve any more solid.

Seismic waves   Sound waves travelling underground which reflect off layers of rock. These can be recorded to help show what type of rock is found in a particular area and to study the effects of earthquakes.

Series   The word used to describe electrical things that have been strung together in a single loop. This loop lets electricity flow out of the battery, through each part, then into the battery again.

Shock wave   A disturbance in the air that travels out in all directions. It is a sound wave that is heard as a loud sound when it reaches your ears. The sound of thunder is produced by a shock wave.

Short circuit   A very easy path that electricity can take around a circuit. A wire directly connected to the two terminals of a battery will make a short circuit. Electricity will always take a short circuit when it can.

Solidify   When a liquid changes into a solid, usually by cooling it.

Solubility   A measurement of how much solid (or gas) dissolves in a fixed amount of liquid.

Soluble   A substance that will dissolve in a liquid.

Solution   The mixture that results when a substance dissolves in a liquid.

Source   The place from which sound or light comes, for example the Sun is a source of light and a cassette player is a source of sound. The energy of both sound and light travels by means of waves.

Spectrum   A band of colours that together make up white light but that can sometimes be separated out, for example by raindrops or a prism, into the seven colour regions seen in rainbows – red, orange, yellow, green, blue, indigo and violet.

Speed   How fast something is going. Speed is calculated by dividing distance by time. Average speed is the total distance travelled on a journey divided by the total time taken.

Static electricity   A type of electricity that you can make by rubbing certain things together, for instance a nylon cloth and a plastic ruler. When you do this, you brush electrons off one item and on to another. This gives both objects an electrical 'charge'.

Streamlined   A shape that reduces drag. A fish has a streamlined shape.

Substance   Any kind of matter. A substance can be a solid, a liquid or a gas. A common word for substance is 'stuff'.

Suspension   A mixture made by shaking small insoluble particles with a liquid.

Temperature   A measurement that

describes how hot something is. On the Celsius temperature scale, water freezes at 0°C and boils at 100°C.

Temporary   A change that can be reversed.

Tough   Solids that do not bend easily and that do not break into pieces when struck. The opposite of brittle.

Translucent   A material is translucent if it lets some light through.

Transparent   A material is transparent if it lets nearly all the light through, so you can see through it clearly.

Triboluminescence   The giving out of light from something when it is rubbed, scratched or broken.

Turning force   The strength of a turning effect. The longer a lever, the greater the turning force it can produce. Also called a 'moment'.

Ultrasound   Sounds with very rapid vibrations whose pitch is too high to be heard by humans. Some animals can hear ultrasound.

Unbalanced forces   Forces that cause a change in the motion or shape of an object, because the force acting in one direction is greater than the force acting in the opposite direction.

Upthrust   The upwards force that acts on an object when it is immersed in a fluid. The size of the force is the same as the weight of the fluid that makes way for the object.

Vapour   Another word for gas.

Vibration   Something moving very quickly backwards and forwards. Sound is produced because of vibrations in the air. Sometimes vibrations can be felt as well as heard.

Vocal cords   A pair of membranes found in the larynx, or voice box. When we breathe air into them from the lungs, they vibrate and produce the sound of our voice. This sound varies in pitch, depending on whether the cords vibrate quickly (high sounds) or slowly (low sounds).

Voltage   A measure of the electrical 'push' a battery can give to the electrons flowing around a circuit. This push is measured in volts (V). Most batteries have their voltage written on their casing. A 4.5V battery, for instance, has three times the electrical push of a 1.5V battery.

Volume   A measurement of the amount of space taken up by an object. The unit of volume is the litre (l). One litre is equal to 1000 millilitres (ml). Millilitres are sometimes called cubic centimetres (cm^3).

Wave   A disturbance of the air. Waves travel from a source of sound in all directions. When they reach your ears, you hear a sound. It is useful to picture sound waves travelling through the air like ripples on a pond.

Weight   The force on an object that results when gravity pulls on its mass. A bag of sugar has a mass of 1kg on Earth and 1kg on the Moon. Its weight on Earth is six times its weight on the Moon because gravity on Earth is six times stronger than on the Moon.

Index

Picture Credits